BUT...
Why Did You Stay?

MEKISHA JANE WALKER

But, Why Did You Stay?

© 2020 Mekisha Jane Walker

Printed in the USA

ISBN (Print Version): ISBN- 979-8614376413

DEDICATION

To Grace...
My Beautiful, Sweet, Funny Daughter
who gave me strength when I thought I had none!

ACKNOWLEDGMENTS

My Husband, Todd Trlicek
My Parents – Nancy and Doug Walker
My Sisters – Layla Wolken and Katie Jane Rankin
My Son, Ryan
All my Nieces and Nephews
Gina Holden
Bobby and Julie Schmidt
Stephanie Proffitt
Bill Exley
Jane Waters
Jack Roady
Maile Veach Chatlos
Angel Magouirk Burg
George Tyson
Jill Lansden Connelly
Jennifer "JL" Carpenter
The witnesses who called 911
All the people who provided love and support!

ENDORSEMENTS

If it can happen to her, a capable trial attorney, it can happen to anyone. Mekisha Jane Walker's ground-breaking and thought-provoking memoir has the potential to change the way domestic violence is viewed. Sharing her journey provides a fascinating insight into the confusion and agony women experience at the hands of an abuser, who was once their perfect love. Mekisha's incorporation of photos, video, audio, and court documents makes you feel as if you were actually there. This book will change lives by helping not only victims but also providing a better understanding of abusive relationships so that parents, siblings, and friends can help the woman on her path to regain control of her life.

William T. Harmon, Former Criminal Court Judge, 34 years

Mekisha Jane Walker takes you through her journey; a strong-willed successful attorney by day and a domestic violence victim by night. With her secret revealed, she was faced with the question, "why did you stay?" This is her answer to the question. She is a force to be reckoned with and she has survived to tell her tale. This compelling page-turner is a powerful read that will help eliminate the shame associated with being labeled a victim and that will raise awareness for this dirty secret that so many strong-willed women living with are afraid to talk about.

Jane Waters, Former Domestic Violence Prosecutor and Division Chief with the Harris County DA's Office, 28 years

As a former prosecutor and current criminal trial attorney, Mekisha Jane Walker is a strong, smart, and resourceful woman. She is funny, bold, energetic, engaging, and makes friends wherever she goes. But she hid her shameful secret of domestic abuse and became trapped, unable to break free from the control of her abuser. A secret no more, she now tells her compelling survival story, which provides remarkable insight into the complications of leaving an abuser. This book intimately shows how *any* woman can experience horrible abuse, and yet overcome it.

Jennifer Varela, MSW, LCSW, Special Victim's Bureau, Harris County DA's Office, 25 years

TABLE OF CONTENTS

INTRODUCTION

"It is not the bruises on the body that hurt. It is the wounds of the heart and the scars on the mind." - Aisha Mirza

As little girls, we dream of one day becoming a ballerina, a doctor; or a lawyer. We dream of having it all – a wonderful husband, beautiful children, a dog, the perfect house with a white picket fence. You know, the classic fairy-tale that most little girls fantasize about with their friends. We desire a simple life filled with love, peace, joy, happiness, and great success. As we grow, our imagination takes us on countless journeys through life that we have yet to encounter. Each one of those imagination-filled journeys is brimming with great adventure, healthy relationships, and lucrative careers. Oh, how wonderful it is to experience child-like imaginations where there is no pain, hurt, hate, discomfort, or negative energy. Even when faced with the difficulties of life, children have a resilience to create other worlds.

The day arrives when that little girl is no longer fantasizing but begins a quest to find her knight in shining armor. You are no longer doodling names or drawing stick figures. You no longer imagine a first kiss or first romantic embrace for countless hours. The universe creates a set time for an undeniable encounter that will bring two unsuspecting individuals together. As they approach one another at the destined time, there is an interaction that is explosive and like no other. There is something unique about this individual that

But, Why Did You Stay?

makes you stop and take notice. You exchange phone numbers, and with the first call, casual conversation evolves into countless hours of not wanting to hang up the phone.

The first date is filled with overwhelming nervousness due to unknown expectations. One date turns into ten and ten into twenty. Before long, you are pondering the idea of moving in together. You journey from talking to dating and from dating to living together, so, the next step must be marriage. Can you imagine how many women find themselves in this dilemma? The dilemma of falling in love with the *idea* of the man, without actually getting to know the total man. You fall in love with who and what they allow you to see. The flaws are hidden away in dark crevasses, waiting to pounce at the most unsuspecting time, and failing to look any further, you get lost in their good looks, fashion, the smell of their cologne, their great manners, and how wonderful they make you feel, never wondering if it could all be a façade, never questioning that this could very well be a fairytale with a not-so-happy ending.

In your heart of hearts, he can do no wrong. Everything about him is perfect in the beginning. There are no signs of mental illness or abusive tendencies. He dare not let on to any narcissistic behaviors. All of the "red flags" are hidden away tightly. In the beginning, he is all smiles, coupled with kind words and lots of patience. Not to say that you don't have any issues of your own, but you truly attempt to give him all of who you are. You open your vault and give him full access to your body, heart, mind, and soul without doing a full life check. Not a background check; but a LIFE check.

You fall prey to what he says and fail to put their deeds and actions to the test. After a while, you begin to see little things that you overlooked, and eventually, they become big things. The man who was once very patient becomes short-tempered

14 | P a g e

and distant. He was once gentle and comforting, but out of nowhere, he becomes aggressive and pushy. Words that were once gentle and kind become hateful and rude. Phone calls that were once loving and consistent, become short and cold.

This might not be your story, but it is definitely mine. Maybe you can relate to some things or none at all. The end result of this story is an unhealthy, unhappy relationship that mutates into abuse. Is the abuse the same for everyone? No! It could be verbal, mental, physical, spiritual, emotional, financial, or sexual. Some may experience variations of situational abuse, but what happens when you experience them all at the hands of one man?

What happens when you give your whole self to a man and in return, he gives you Dr. Jekyll and Mr. Hyde? You have no idea who you are going to wake up to from day to day. You live in despair and walk on eggshells for fear of awakening the beast. You find yourself questioning your very existence and wondering how much longer you will live. Your emotions are so twisted and entangled that you rationalize between leaving and staying because he plays on your heart through guilt. These are real encounters that women live with and through day after day. Some are fortunate to escape, and some are not. I was fortunate to escape...but I barely made it out! The quote at the beginning says, *"It is not the bruises on the body that hurt. It is the wounds of the heart and the scars on the mind."*

Though I suffered many bruises on my body, they eventually healed and are no longer visible to the human eye. But my heart and my mind went unhealed for many years. I smiled on the outside, but my heart was frowning. I dressed up, went to work, and took care of my kids, all the while still possessing a wounded soul.

Today, I choose to share my truth, because God chose me to survive so that others could hear my journey and escape. So many times, I have been asked the dreaded question, "But, why did you stay?" To be honest, you can't assume how you'll respond in a given situation until put in that situation. As I share the gruesome details of my story, it is my hope that you will find the strength to overcome any negative situation that is hindering your life. Yours might not be abuse, but it could be something negative that is causing you pain or discomfort. I hope friends, brothers, sisters, and parents use my story to educate themselves and their loved ones, so they can spot the red flags that so often go unnoticed.

My overall hope for this book is that it helps others discover the importance of loving and choosing SELF, and knowing that abuse is not your fault, but it is your problem. A problem that must be dealt with before it's too late.

Note:

As you prepare to dive into the pages of this book, it was my desire to make my experience as real to you as possible. With that being said, Visit www.butwhydidyoustay.com, my interactive website, that chronicles the indepthness of each individual chapter with photos, videos, transcripts, news articles, and live voice recordings.

CHAPTER ONE

The End Before the Beginning

I t was a crisp night, perfect for the Harris County Criminal Lawyers Association Annual Christmas party. As I stood in the mirror with my new dress on, I couldn't help but notice how wonderful I looked. Just five months prior, I had given birth to our daughter, Gracie. Despite a little leftover baby weight, I looked and felt amazing! Once my husband, Luke, laid eyes on me, I just knew he was going to compliment how I looked, but unfortunately, that wasn't the case.

Mom was babysitting, so we had to drop Gracie off at her house. Even my mother couldn't help but notice how stunning I looked. She asked, "Luke, doesn't she look beautiful?" He patted me on the belly and rubbed it in small circles while saying, "Why, yes she does!" This was as close to an unsolicited compliment as I was ever going to get. I smiled sweetly and touched his hand as I said, "Thank you!"

When we got to the party, I looked for people I recognized, but it was still early. We made our way to the buffet area where I got some appetizers, but nothing appealed to Luke, so he went to the bar instead. We both agreed that we were not going to stay out late, but after a few drinks, Luke wanted to stay. He was talking to another elected official and having a good time.

I was standing next to Luke when I felt someone playfully slap me on the butt as they walked by. As I turned around in disarray, I recognized the person as Scott Fisher, a prosecutor with the Harris County District Attorney's office, someone I had only interacted within the courtroom. I never had contact with him outside work and didn't even have his phone number. I had no idea why he slapped me on the ass.

When Luke saw what happened, he went into a complete rage. He demanded to know who Scott was. I told him he was a prosecutor. He started yelling, "Who does he think he is, that he can just slap another man's wife on the ass?" He was furious! He had every right to be, but his explosive reaction was embarrassing. After many years of verbal outbursts, I knew that this could escalate and very quickly.

Luke went on and on about how disrespectful it was for Scott to slap my ass while he was standing right there. Luke took the valet ticket, ensuring I couldn't leave without him. He forced me to walk around the club and look for Scott. I walked past Scott several times acting like I didn't see him because I didn't want there to be a physical confrontation between the two. I repeatedly begged to leave, but Luke refused.

At this point, many people were starting to notice that something was going on, which made me feel really uncomfortable. So, I went outside and explained to the valet guy that my husband was inside drunk and that I needed my car keys. The valet acted like this was not the first time he heard a story like this, and he opened the box of keys. I reached in and grabbed mine. The valet walked me to my car, and I thanked him.

Everything in me wanted to drive away, but I knew the consequences of that choice would not end well. Even if I left him and he got home another way, I would still have to endure the physical, verbal, and mental abuse from his raging anger. I didn't cause this anger, but I knew I would suffer the wrath of it. I called my mom to get her advice. I told her what happened at the party, and that I was thinking about leaving Luke there. She reasoned that he was my husband and that I shouldn't just leave him stranded all the way across town. While that made sense to her at the time, I know her answer would have been different had she known what our relationship was truly like.

I called my friend and co-worker, Cary from the car. She was inside the party, so I told her to find Scott and tell him to stay away from Luke. I then called Luke's best friend, James, and told him that I was about to leave Luke and that he would have to come and get Luke. James, who was a police officer, told me that he had to work early in the morning and that I should call, another friend, Shane. So, I called Shane and was explaining the situation when Luke started calling me repeatedly. I told Shane that I had to answer the other line and that I would call him back. I was scared and my heart was beating like it was going to jump out of my chest. I didn't want to ride home with Luke under any circumstances because I knew he was angry, and his anger would soon be directed at me.

When I clicked over, Luke promised that he wouldn't take his anger out on me and that nothing was going to happen. I was really skeptical, but I felt I had no other option. So, I drove to the turnaround where Luke was standing. He walked toward the vehicle, opened the driver's side door and told me he was driving. I told him he was drunk and didn't need to be behind the wheel. He said, "I drive better drunk than you do sober!"

When I walked around to get into the passenger side, I saw Cary and she said, "See you tomorrow!" With a very blank stare, I replied, "Maybe!" I don't know why I said this; I see her every day. At that moment, an eerie feeling came over me. My emotions were running rampant, and my body was nearly numb due to the fear of the unknown. I wanted so much to believe his promise that he wouldn't hurt me, but I also knew him and how violent he was. In my gut, I knew something terrible was going to happen.

As we drove away from the club, Luke told me he was driving me to the Houston Police Department substation to file assault charges against Scott. "Really?" I thought. After all the assaults I had suffered at HIS hands, he wanted me to file charges for a playful slap on the ass. It was absurd! I objected and said, "I am not going to file a police report for assault against someone that I have to work with every day."

Luke looked at me with fierce anger in his eyes and screamed, "You're fucking him, aren't you?" Totally appalled by this erroneous allegation, I couldn't even open my mouth to respond before he took my phone and broke it. I tried to convince him that nothing was happening between Scott and me, but he continued to insist that I would file a report. He said, "Yes you will!" and I said, "No, I won't!"

We continued arguing back and forth until out of nowhere Luke backhanded me, hitting me in the nose with his fist. My head slammed back against the headrest, and blood started pouring out my nose. I cupped my hands underneath my nose in an attempt to catch all the blood but was unsuccessful for the most part. In an arrogant, abusive tone, he said, "You gonna file one now?" With tears streaming down my face, I instantly responded, "Yes, yes I will!" The pain that came from the punch was very familiar. At that moment, I became even more numb. I damn near felt like I was having an out of body experience. I was shaking and praying to just get home, knowing that it would soon be over. I thought he would yell at me and maybe hit me a couple more times. Then, as usual, I would clean myself up, go to sleep, and be grateful that I lived to see another day.

Well, on this particular night, it didn't quite happen the way I expected. Luke pulled into a parking lot and started to drive behind a restaurant, into this dark, dead-end dumpster area. As he was turning toward this dark area, I had to think quickly, but because I was afraid of what would happen next. Luke broke my personal cell phone, but I remembered I still had my work cell phone and grabbed it. No matter what was about to happen, I needed a way to communicate.

An overwhelming and unexplainable gut feeling convinced me that I had to get away before he made it to the dead end. He was driving slowly through the parking lot, and at the same time my heart was racing, my thoughts scattered, and my adrenaline was pumping hard. I carefully lifted the inside door lock, trying not to alert him, but I failed. I planned to open the door, step out onto the running board, and then run in the opposite direction.

This seemed like the perfect plan until he noticed me manually unlocking the door. In a panic, I reached for the door handle and opened the door. As I put my foot on the running board and stood to get out of the car, Luke turned the wheel and punched the accelerator. I fell out of the car and hit the ground headfirst. My forehead smacked the concrete, split open, and blood gushed everywhere. I had envisioned my death at the hands of Luke numerous times, but I never imagined anything like this. At that moment, I was certain that my life was over. There are absolutely NO words to describe the fear and panic that accompanies believing you are about to die. I didn't feel the physical pain, because the adrenaline was off the charts, pumping rapidly through my body.

I lay there on the ground in a pool of my own blood, and Luke drove away and left me. I heard a voice telling me to "get up" and "run for help." This voice overwhelmed me, and I found the strength to get up. I struggled to move, but the adrenaline masked the pain. On the other side of the parking lot, I saw a man and I ran towards him, collapsing in the grass.

I remember the man trying to help me while screaming for others to call 9-1-1 and get a towel. Before long I was surrounded by people, which should have made me feel better, but it didn't. All I could think about was what was going to happen next. I heard the man on the phone with 9-1-1 telling the operator that I had been run over by a car. I tried to tell him what had happened, but someone else was holding me down and telling me to be quiet and stop talking. Then, unbelievably, Luke returned to the scene and drove the car towards me. I immediately panicked and started screaming bloody murder because I was certain he was going to run me over and finish me off, but he stopped just short of the crowd.

He got out of the car aggressively and said, "I'm a police officer; this was an accident." Thankfully, another witness took the keys out of the ignition, and Luke was then faced with what he had done. Luke looked at him and said, "You'll be sorry. I'll get your name from the court records." Instead of staying there with me, Luke chose to run away on foot from the scene, knowing the police were on the way.

As I laid there on the ground waiting for the ambulance, I called Cary, because I had just seen her and knew she was still close by. I told her, "Something has happened, and I need you to come over here!" She came right away and rode with me in the ambulance to the hospital. During the ride, she asked me what happened. I told her the truth. She said, "You have to tell the police what happened!" I told her that I couldn't. I feared what Luke would do. I feared for myself and my family.

I called my mom and gave her instructions. I told her to get her gun and to take Gracie somewhere where Luke would not find either of them. Of course, she had questions, but I told her I would explain more later. Then I called another friend and asked her to pick up our older son, Ryan, from our house. I was trying to work through in my mind what Luke's next move would be. I came up with two options. He would either rent a hotel room and shoot himself, or he would go on some kind of killing rampage that could include our children.

The paramedics overheard all my phone conversations and relayed what they heard to the police officers. There I was, in the back of an ambulance on the way to the hospital with my life flashing before me, all because I fell in love with the wrong person. All because I chose to remain in a relationship that had shattered my very existence for years. That choice could now cost me my life. My choice could cause me to never see my beautiful baby girl, Ryan, or any of my family again.

You ask me, "But, why did you stay?" The answer to this question is more difficult to explain than you'd think. For the longest time, I dreaded the question because the answer is not simple. If I had disclosed my secret, I would have had support from family and more friends than I could count, which is more than most women can say. I was the breadwinner and not forced to stay for financial reasons, unlike too many.

Depending on *when* in the relationship you asked, "But, why did you stay?" I would give a different answer. In the beginning, I stayed because I loved him, and I believed I could help him change. For better or for worse.... Toward the end, love morphed to fear that overcame my ability to get out of the relationship. I was absolutely convinced that he would make good on his threat to kill me, Gracie, my mom or my sister. I stayed out of absolute terror.

If I didn't actually live through the traumatic abuse, I would love to say it was all a dream or a long nightmare that never seemed to end. I lived in hell on earth for years and most of those years I suffered in silence. I covered up the bruises and scars with expensive makeup. I used scarves to hide his handprints on my neck. I became the master of disguise and, I must admit, I became rather good at it.

But the time came when small bruises turned into big bruises. Making love, became forced, unwanted sex. Simple text messages between a husband and a wife went from kind words to a reply with a picture of his gun, no words. As I unpack my story piece by piece, moment by moment, and memory by memory, it will become more and more evident that love is blind, fear is tormenting, and domestic violence should never be condoned under any circumstances.

Love shouldn't hurt...ever.

But hindsight is 20/20, as they say. This is one final incident of many that led to the end of a dreadful chapter in my life while opening the door to new beginnings.

Visit www.butwhydidyoustay.com my interactive website, that chronicles the indepthness of each individual chapter with photos, videos, transcripts, news articles, and live voice recordings.

CHAPTER TWO

My Knight in Shining Armor

My name is Mekisha Jane Walker and today I am a loving wife, a mother of two, and an attorney. But, before I took on all these great roles, I was simply Mekisha...a white girl, with a black girl name, as many like to point out. I was bullied in school and learned just how cruel kids could be. I'm sure you can only imagine the things they said, but it didn't make me timid. It actually built my character, made me stronger, and taught me how to not care what others thought.

In elementary school, my parents moved us from a not so great part of Houston to Clear Lake, a well to do Houston suburb full of lawyers, doctors, and astronauts. This transition was particularly difficult for me because my parents didn't have the money to buy me the designer clothes all the other kids had. I vividly remember begging for a pair of Guess jeans, because they were all the rage in the '80s. One pair of Guess jeans nearly cost what my mom spent on school clothes for the entire year. So clearly, I didn't get the jeans, and it was embarrassing to wear my off-brand clothes surrounded by everyone in the name-brand clothes.

From a young age, I tried to earn my own money. I would knock on doors and ask if I could weed neighbors' flower beds. When I got older, I took up babysitting. I also had a gig selling candy door to door. At fifteen, I was finally old enough to get a real job, sacking groceries at Kroger. My parents co-signed a bank loan to get me a used car, and I paid that note monthly.

I have always had a job, even through college and law school. My mother always told my sisters and me, "You have to go to college, so you won't have to depend on a man for support." We all listened!

Throughout my life, I learned how situations and circumstances test our character and build our strength. I must say I certainly had my fair share of situations, especially in the area of relationships. I experienced relationship woes right out of high school. During high school, a friend from the restaurant where I worked, introduced me to his friend, Sean. Sean was home on a two-week leave from boot camp, and we spent the majority of it together. He was then stationed in Germany. He loved to receive letters from me, so I wrote and mailed him at least one letter daily, that I usually wrote during English class.

We corresponded and flew back and forth over the next two years. I graduated high school and just a year after that, we got married and moved to Savannah, Georgia, where he was stationed. When unpacking boxes one day, I discovered an entire box full of my letters, all unopened! I was so hurt and when I confronted him, he apologized. There were signs, but it wasn't until he completely stopped coming home at night that I knew he was cheating on me.

It took some time, but I moved back home and continued in my undergraduate studies. My younger sister, Layla, also married a year out of high school, and over twenty-five years later, they are still happily married. Their wedding was around the time that I started dating my brother-in-law's best friend, Greg. Greg and I dated for four years and were engaged when I started law school. But our relationship didn't survive my first year of law school.

One day I was studying for finals when Greg came over and told me that he was breaking up with me because he had been seeing someone else and she was pregnant. I blamed myself because I didn't pay him enough attention. I was so hurt, but I didn't really have time to think about it. I immersed myself in law school, spending the majority of my time working on law review and national moot court championships.

I have always been very loyal and "Mrs. Fix It" for everything and everybody, so I didn't understand why my relationships failed. I questioned myself, wondering if I was the reason for my failed relationships. I had dates here and there, but nothing serious. When I graduated from law school in 2002, I was ecstatic to receive a pre-commit position as an Assistant District Attorney for Harris County. This had been my dream since seventh grade, and it was now a reality.

Achieving this, I should have felt complete, but I was lonely. One night, I was out with some of my guy friends from law school. We attended a comedy show in Downtown Houston. After the show, we walked over to a nightclub, called the Mercury Room. When we entered the club, I couldn't help but notice this very handsome guy standing near the entrance. He instantly caught my attention, not only because he was good looking but, also because he looked good in his Harris County Sheriff's Department uniform. He was working an extra job at the club as security. I immediately commented to one of my guy friends that I thought he was super cute. I wanted to walk over and strike up a conversation, but I didn't want to do it alone and none of the guys would go with me. So, I needed some girl power! I called a girlfriend, told her that I needed her to come up there.

I waited outside for her, and she arrived a few minutes later. By that time, the cute guy was working the front door, checking ID's. My friend and I got in line together. We intentionally had our driver's licenses next to our District Attorney badges so that he would notice. We just knew that would spark up a conversation, and it did. We stood outside and talked for a while. When I told him I had to leave, he asked if he could get my phone number to call me sometime.

He texted me the next day and asked me to dinner. I remember telling a secretary at work that I had met the man of my dreams over the weekend. I didn't have any doubts, and this was before we had our first date. We went to dinner a couple of days later and really hit it off. The attraction was indescribable.

Then the next night, we went out again to a movie and after that, we started to see each other regularly, almost daily. After the other failed relationships, I was hesitant, but he was different. He was attentive to a level I had not experienced before. The conversation was always about me. He was always checking on me, holding my hand and treating me like a princess. He put me on a pedestal that I didn't want to come down from. This was like my own fairytale come true. He was my knight in shining armor.

I fell in love so quickly that looking back it is downright scary. Today, I realize that I fell in love with the way he treated me and how he made me feel because I had no clue who he really was in that short amount of time. I hadn't even learned everything about him. Nor had he learned everything about me. Like they say, "Love is blind" and in this case, I wasn't seeing the full picture. Within just a few weeks, we moved in together.

It was March of 2003. I was a young prosecutor, and he was a police officer. Everyone thought I was crazy for moving so quickly, but I didn't care. For me, it felt right, and I wasn't going to allow anyone to talk me out of this perfect opportunity. My emotions were totally in control because truth be told, I wasn't thinking at all.

Soon, I found out that he had a four-year-old son named Ryan, who lived with his mom's aunt. Quite naturally, I was curious about why his son wasn't living with him. Luke told me he worked nights, making it impossible for him to have full-time custody. While I totally understood his dilemma, I told him that I didn't want to be in a relationship with someone who was not a part of their child's life. He heard me loud and clear and the next day Ryan was living with us full-time. We created an instant family.

When I think back after the healing process, I can honestly say that I was trying to fill a void. Both of my younger sisters were having babies. I achieved my professional goals, but my personal life had suffered in the process. I wanted to settle down and have a lifetime partner. The timing of this new relationship couldn't have been more perfect. I just knew that Luke was "the one."

Looking back, I see that I fell in love with the image of the man Luke allowed me to see, not the person he truly was. He had some deep emotional scars lying dormant beneath his surface and before I knew it, they began revealing themselves one after the other.

Shortly after we moved in together, some law school friends invited us on a trip to go floating down the river. We all chipped in to stay at a cozy little bed and breakfast. It was the cutest little house with a campfire in the back.

The plan was to arrive on a Friday, go floating on Saturday and drive back on Sunday. I was extremely excited, but Luke seemed particularly irritated by the close friendships I had, especially with the men in our group. It didn't matter to him that the males were with their significant others. This was clearly a sign that something wasn't right. Sirens started to ring in my head and my heart, but I ignored them.

After dinner the first night, he said the trip was a bad idea and that he wanted to go home. Since we were already there, I convinced him to go floating on the river. We had already spent the money for the trip, so why not enjoy it?

Anyone who's ever floated on an inner tube down a river knows it's difficult to control which direction you drift, or how fast you go and sometimes you get separated, causing you to float in front of (or behind) other people. When my tube wasn't close enough to him, Luke got pissed off. I was still within visible sight, with no control of the float, but to him, it was unacceptable that we weren't right next to each other. He motioned for me to paddle back closer to him. I was paddling the whole time instead of floating. It was absolutely absurd.

At one point, we used our toes to hold on to each other and my toes slipped, causing me to float away faster than he did. This made him even angrier. I was grabbing onto tree branches trying to stop myself, so he could catch up with me. This went on for hours. He was visibly pissed off the whole time and never spoke to anyone. By the end of the float, he was no longer speaking to me. It was very awkward because everyone could tell that something was wrong. When we got back to the bed-and-breakfast, everyone gathered around the campfire to hang out, but he refused. He made me get dinner for him and bring it up to the room. I just wanted to enjoy myself and relax, but that wasn't going to happen no matter what I did.

We had an argument about leaving and driving home that night versus waking up in the morning and driving home. After arguing for hours about leaving, I finally convinced him that it was too late to drive home and that we should just spend the night and leave in the morning. I was hoping that the next morning he would be out of his bad mood, but he wasn't. He woke me up and while everyone was sleeping, we left without saying goodbye to anyone.

I should've known that something was wrong with him, but instead, I interpreted this as him liking me so much that he couldn't stand not being right next to me. Boy, was I wrong! This had nothing to do with me and everything to do with him and his emotional issues that were slowly being revealed. Today, I understand that men who are abusive are very territorial and they work hard to get you isolated from family and friends. I had worked on domestic violence cases, and had been educated on "the signs," but they aren't as easy to spot when you experience them for yourself.

Before we were married, I purchased our first house. It was a great starter home, located in Clear Lake. The house was just one block over from the house where I lived during elementary and middle school. So, this made our new home feel even more like home. Shortly after we moved in, we were scheduled to go to Maile's wedding. She had been my best friend since the fifth grade and there was no way I would miss her wedding day. Luke agreed to go, but he wasn't very happy about the trip.

We flew to Aiken, South Carolina for the rehearsal dinner and ceremony. Luke did not make a good impression at the rehearsal dinner. He appeared bored, unapproachable and wouldn't talk to anyone. When we got back to the hotel, he demanded we fly home because he didn't like it there. Clearly, I wasn't going anywhere. I was going to be there for my best friend. The fact that I chose her over his comfort, put him in a permanently bad mood.

The next day, I was scheduled to be at the beauty salon most of the day with all the other girls in the wedding party. The groom invited Luke to hang out with the guys on the golf course. Luke refused; claiming it would be awkward since he didn't know any of them. Instead, he came with me to the beauty salon. This was very annoying because it was supposed to be an all-day, all-girl hangout. He felt the vibe from some of the girls, so he went outside and sat on a bench, where he began incessantly texting me about how he wanted to leave. Even Maile went out and tried to talk to him, but he insisted on pouting on the bench all day.

When we went back to the hotel room to get dressed for the wedding, he threatened to break up with me if I didn't agree to go home with him right then. He was checking flight times. I told him I wasn't leaving, and he could do what he wanted. I couldn't even enjoy being with my best friend on her wedding day because I was dealing with all of his drama. When he saw I wasn't budging, he ended up relenting and going to the wedding. He made the evening miserable for me with his horrid attitude.

These events are just a fraction of what I endured in the beginning. They were enormous signs for me to run in the opposite direction, but like many women, I thought I could *love the hell out of him.* I wanted to help him conquer his issues, without ever realizing the toll it was costing me emotionally.

I tried to rationalize his behavior by thinking about his horrible childhood. He grew up in poverty and he watched, through the slats of the closet door, as his mother had sex with men for money, at least this is what he told me. I wondered how a mother could do this to their child. When Luke was eight years old, he found a phone number for the man whom his mother claimed was his biological father. He called the number and the man told Luke that he was not his father and to never call him again.

When Luke was about eight, she became pregnant again, this time with twins! When the twins were thirteen months old, she gave them up for adoption because the financial burden became too great. Luke was devastated and full of resentment toward his mother. Then, when Luke was eleven, she died of cancer. Because of his traumatic childhood experiences, he had a love-hate memory of his mother.

Luke was then raised by her brother, who according to Luke was horrible to him — physically and verbally abusing him, and constantly reminding Luke that he was only putting a roof over his head because that was the promise he made to his dying sister. Later, I found out that Luke's uncle called him the "blue-eyed devil."

I felt so bad that Luke had such a horrible childhood. No dad, dead mom, and then, growing up without someone who actually loved him. I was convinced that I could love him and make him forget the pain of his past. I would show him what love felt like and make up for all he had been through. At least that was my intention. Looking back, I was so naive to think I could fix him with love. He was way too damaged. He hid the damage, releasing it slowly, piece by piece. No matter how hard a person tries, some people can't be fixed with only love.

But, Why Did You Stay?

CHAPTER THREE

The Warnings I Ignored

Shortly after Luke and I moved in together, I got an excruciating migraine. I have suffered from migraines since I was a teenager. I have one almost every day of varying degrees. Rarely, I will get one so severe that I feel like I am going to die. Nausea accompanies these severe headaches, which eventually leads to vomiting. Once the vomiting begins, I refer to this as "the point of no return." The vomiting continues until I'm only throwing up blood. The only way to come back from these rare occasions is to go to the hospital and get anti-nausea medication, IV liquids, and sleep it off.

On this particular occasion, Luke woke up in the middle of the night to find me lying on the bathroom floor, having just vomited and crying, "I want my mommy." He told me that I was a grown woman and that it was ridiculous for me to say I wanted my mother. He continued to scold me that I needed to get up because it was nasty to lay on the floor. I got back in bed and tried to endure the pain, but very quickly had to run back to the toilet to throw up more blood.

After that, I decided to call my mother to have her take me to the hospital. When he found out that I called my mother, he said, "If you have your mother drive over here in the middle of the night, we're breaking up." I could hardly think; the pain was intense. I saw Mom pull up, and I ran outside without telling him I was leaving.

When I got to the emergency room, I immediately laid down on the cold floor; it felt nice and cool after vomiting repeatedly. I did not care if it was "nasty." My mother understood. She sat on the ground next to me and rubbed my forehead. She knew just what I needed.

Right before they took me back to a room, Luke showed up. This was the first time he and my mother met. What a great first impression! He told Mom she could leave, but of course, she didn't leave. The doctor did his usual evaluation and ordered some anti-nausea medicine and fluids, which helped bring the pain down to a tolerable level.

About an hour later, I was released. I could tell that Luke was still mad about the whole situation, but it was out of my control. We all walked out to the parking lot. I thanked my mom for coming and got in the car with Luke to go back home.

I should have known right then that there was something wrong with him. He had no empathy whatsoever. He could in no way relate to my pain. This was not the same man who wooed me with attention. This wasn't love! But in my desire to be loyal to who I thought he was, I dismissed my concern and tried to convince myself that he just didn't "get it" because he didn't understand how debilitating a migraine could actually be. I convinced myself this was an isolated incident. Over time, this proved to be far from the truth. In the beginning, these instances of him behaving horribly were isolated. The good times far out-weighed the bad, and I loved my new family.

In January 2005, we took our relationship a step further and got married. Although we moved in together quickly, I waited almost two years before marriage. So, I felt like I had given the relationship enough time to be sure I was making the right decision. Our wedding day was beautiful, and I enjoyed every moment of it. But, shortly after professing our love to one another and reciting our vows in front of friends and family, something shifted. Or, maybe I should say, the *real* Luke showed up. He was showing signs of dysfunction before the wedding, but these signs didn't prepare me for what happened next. I had no clue what my life was about to become.

We paid for the entire wedding and honeymoon with our own money. Since we had to pay for all of this on top of living expenses, we tried to cut corners and do our honeymoon on a budget. We decided on a Disney World honeymoon. To save money, we booked a hotel that wasn't located on the Disney property. Based on the pictures from the website, the hotel appeared to be a lavish resort. However, when we arrived, we discovered it was really an apartment complex they were calling a "resort." Although it was not what I expected, I was fine with it because it was spacious, clean and the Disney shuttle bus came by. Luke, on the other hand, was very upset. He said he didn't want to stay in some "ghetto" place on our honeymoon.

I understood where he was coming from, but we had already spent too much money. I was prepared to make the best of it. I was just happy that we were together and that's all that mattered to me at that moment. He was acting like he was too good to stay in a place that didn't have a concierge desk. These were the beginning signs of seeing just how self-absorbed he truly was.

Luke spent most of the first day trying to get us moved to a hotel on Disney property. Ultimately, he chose the nicest and most expensive hotel and booked a suite on the top floor. The hotel was fabulous, but I felt guilty because it was going to take us forever to pay off that credit card debt.

When we finally got situated, we were so exhausted that we both fell asleep. We woke up the next morning and we were in the middle of making love when there was a knock at the door. The voice on the other side said, "Housekeeping." Luke told me to say something, but I didn't know what to say and didn't respond quickly enough. Suddenly, the door opened. The man was about to come in when he quickly realized the room was occupied. He turned around and immediately walked out. Luke jumped off me without finishing and yelled, "You ruined everything!" "Me?" I thought, "How could I ruin anything when you're the one who stopped?" But I didn't say anything.

I did my best to enjoy the remainder of our honeymoon, but it wasn't easy, there was constant tension. There were so many questions running through my mind. I didn't want another failed marriage, so I made up my mind right then that I would love him, and I would make our marriage work. Little did I know, this incident was a preview of emotions I would come to live with daily for many years.

After the honeymoon, Luke decided he wanted to go to law school; he studied for the admissions test and I helped him fill out all his applications and wrote his personal statement. Unfortunately, Luke was not accepted to any local law schools, but he did receive a letter that he was on the wait-list for South Texas College of Law in Houston, the same school I graduated from. This meant he would only be admitted if other accepted students declined. He was extremely disappointed. So, I went to visit one of the Deans who agreed to look into it. The next day, Luke was accepted as a law student at South Texas College of Law.

Not long after the wedding, I was experiencing a plethora of emotions about several different things that were happening in my life. I had a new husband. I had a new son. I was working hard in my career, and then life shifted once again. This time it was my Grandma Jane. Growing up as a little girl, she and I were very close and alike in many ways. We understood and appreciated our similarities. I loved her so much, proven by the fact that I would sneak Whataburger (extra onion) into the nursing home. She wasn't supposed to have it, but she really enjoyed it and I loved breaking the rules.

By 2006, her cancer came back with a vengeance and took her. I was holding her hand when she took her last breath. Her time in hospice and her death caused me to reflect on how much time I was giving my job. There were so many Sunday family dinners and other family events that I missed because I was preparing for trials that ended up getting reset or not going for one reason or another.

When I first started as a prosecutor, people tried to tell me to slow down or I would burn out. My reply was always, "I'm Mekisha, I don't burn out." But when my Grandma Jane passed, I realized that I wasn't making the difference that I thought I was. I realized that if I quit, they would just move someone else in my position. This person wouldn't work as hard as I did, but no one would care. After I came to this realization, I decided I wanted to leave the DA's office. Without a plan, I turned in my two weeks' notice. I decided if some of the attorneys I dealt with on a daily basis, could make a living, then surely, I could. So, the same month Grandma passed, I quit my job and started my own law firm. This was around the same time Luke enrolled in law school, so it became a very stressful time for everyone.

Grandma Jane wanted me to have a baby so badly, but I was focused on my career and wanted to wait for the right time. After she passed, I was devastated she would never hold or see my baby. So, Luke and I decided we would try to get pregnant. When I didn't get pregnant quickly, I feared I was too old to have a baby. So, we started seeing a fertility doctor who checked both Luke and me and told us everything looked fine. When I knew it was possible for us to conceive, I wondered when, and if, it would happen. Eventually, when I still didn't conceive, we saved up for fertility treatments.

I cashed in my county retirement to supplement my income until I established a client base and started bringing in some money. Less than a month later, Luke came home from work and told me that he had turned in his two weeks' notice that night. We had not discussed this at all, and his resignation was a complete surprise to me. He said that he couldn't go to law school and work, that it was just too much. I was shocked! We went from a two-income family to just me! I was now responsible for the mortgage, two car notes, daycare, all our credit cards and everything else that came up. The honeymoon was definitely over.

Luke refused to curb his spending even though we were down to one income, and this didn't help our relationship. When he got mad about me commenting on the finances, he would punch the wall or break something sentimental to me. Anyone who knows me can attest to just how sentimental I am (and that I save everything).

One day, he took a small vase Grandma Jane had given me years before and smashed it into small pieces. I tried picking up the pieces, with the intention of gluing it back together, but there were just too many. Whenever he felt pressure, he would break something he knew I treasured. Although I was very displeased with this behavior, I found myself excusing his behavior because he wasn't being violent with me. But I wasn't able to use this warped theory for long.

Everyone knows your phone must be on silent in the courtroom. Out of habit, I would religiously turn my ringer off before walking into the courthouse. One day, I left court and walked the three blocks to my office. I had a client meeting and forgot to turn my ringer back on. When my client left, I looked down at my phone to see that Luke had called and texted me numerous times. I walked out of my office, and I saw Luke standing on the street right in front of me. I was shocked to see him. He wasn't working, so there was no logical reason for him to be near my office in downtown Houston.

I could tell he was extremely pissed. He walked up to me and started yelling at the top of his lungs, asking me if I was fucking someone inside my office. I froze because I was totally caught off guard and horrified that someone, I knew would see him screaming at me. Trying to calm him down, I told him that I wasn't doing anything wrong. He looked at me and said, "You're a dirty lying bitch!" Then he took his wedding ring off and threw it into the street. I hadn't done anything to warrant this type of reaction. I was in complete disbelief. Trying to prove my love for him, I ran across three lanes of traffic to pick up his ring and bring it back to him.

I wanted everything to be okay and for Luke to feel secure. I pleaded with him to forgive me and begged him to put his ring back on. Now I see, he was slowly, but surely, chipping away my dignity. I was a strong woman who fought in courtrooms and advocated for others. But to get past this very embarrassing moment, I apologized so the argument would not continue at home.

I often wondered if I made the wrong decision marrying Luke, but I felt like I was too far in to turn back. How could I face my family and friends knowing that I jumped into this without really getting to know him? I chalked up a lot of his behavior to the stress of law school. I mean, I knew just how stressful law school was. I thought if I was supportive, it would get our marriage through this difficult time and then everything would be better. But the thought lingered in my mind, "Your husband is supposed to love and protect, not intentionally cause you pain by breaking your things and calling you a fat whore. So, if he can do these things, what else is he capable of?" Before long, my thoughts would become a painful reality.

CHAPTER FOUR

A Life Revolving Around Him

In the beginning of our relationship, before we were married, there was not any physical or verbal abuse. The transition to physical didn't begin until after we were married and happened so gradually, I barely noticed. He would grab or push me, but it wasn't like he was hitting or punching me. His verbal abuse broke me mentally, and I forgave him after each incident. Each time, I wanted so badly to believe his promise that it would never happen again.

Everything seemed like it revolved around Luke- what *he* wanted, how *he* felt, what *he* thought was right. I was just *there*, at his beck and call, making things happen and, to be honest, receiving very little in return.

Not long after moving into our first house, my law practice was doing better, which meant an increase in finances. Luke was no longer satisfied with our starter home, and he insisted we move into a more expensive house in a prestigious neighborhood down the street. He was obsessed with appearances.

Since I was still the only one working, I suggested we wait until he started working again. He refused to listen to reason. He was convinced that the housing market was hot and that we should act right then and there. To keep the peace, I agreed, and we started looking for another house. We purchased our home in my name only because his credit would not allow us to qualify for the loan together.

It was in 2007, before the housing market crashed, and shockingly, I was able to qualify for a $350,000 house with "stated income." This was the worst financial decision I ever made. The monthly note was way beyond what we could afford, but Luke always wanted to live like we were rich.

One night, Luke tried to smother me with a pillow. I woke up from a deep sleep freaking out and believing I was about to die. Before bed, I always put lotion on my wrists and hands, which helped me pull free from his grip. All I could think about was the pain it would cause my family to find me dead. Luke had taken a bunch of Ambien and insisted he was just playing around.

Over the years, Luke constantly reminded me that no one would ever believe I was abused because I had never reported it, so I started keeping a journal. Prior to this, I never kept a journal, but I felt compelled to document what was happening. Because nothing was ever his fault, this journal was my way to feel like I was talking to someone, without having to share my secret unhappiness, which would be far too embarrassing. I could not bring myself to confide in anyone that I allowed Luke to treat me the way he did. The abuse was real, but he always tried to flip the script and blame me for every abusive encounter.

One of my first journal entries on 6/30/2008 read as follows:

6/30/2008

Last night was the worst night of my life. The checking account went down to $513 and I transferred $1000 from the business account, but still that was very little money. I told Luke. We talked about what to do, options. Letting the house go into foreclosure or putting it up for sale, etc. Then Luke announced he was going to get an apartment and leave, so he wouldn't have to worry about all this anymore. I told him, "I knew you would leave." He snapped and came at me in a rage. I was lying on the bed under the covers and I froze in fear. I knew it was useless to try and get away. He put his hand over my mouth and yelled, "Shut up or I'll fucking kill you." He asked me, "Do you want to die?" I shook my head no and whimpered. He took his other hand and grinded my glasses into my face until they were bent and mangled and then threw them to the side. I didn't move. I knew if I did it would make him more mad and the beating would be worse when I was caught. So, I stayed. He mounted me and punched me in the stomach. Then he punched me in the left side of my head, in the hair area above my ear. These two punches were quick. He was smashing down on my mouth with his other hand telling me to shut up. The pain was horrible, but it hurts worse now. I think I was in shock then. I was freaking out. He went for the gun and said, "This is going to be a murder/suicide." I screamed, "No, please!" He said, "I'm going to kill your mom, so you can really understand what pain is." I tried to scream, but he had his hand over my mouth. He agreed to let go, if I agreed shut up. He came out of the rage. I saw the transformation on his face. He asked me if I was going to call the police. I looked in the mirror. To my disbelief, I didn't have any marks. I told him it would be my word against his. He said, that he would tell the police the truth. I knew he was lying. I knew he was telling me this so I would forgive him. I knew that if the police were called, a case would be filed in Harris County and it would be the talk of the courthouse. I think I'd rather be beaten again than be exposed that way. So, I did nothing, like I always do. Nothing! He calmed so quickly it was freaky. He felt bad for what he'd done and blamed it on PTSD, his mother being dead and never knowing his father. I suggested that *maybe there was some medication he could take. He insisted he said he couldn't be fixed, and he was always going to be this way. The past times he's hurt me, he usually just "roughs me up" by throwing me around, pushing, pulling, shoving, twisting arms and wrists, pulling hair and choking. He tells me that he can kill me with his bare hands and that one-day I'll be dead. He gets so mad that he's in a zone, like he is not even Luke, the funny, sweet man I fell in love with.*

This was one of many journal entries that documented the abuse I was experiencing in silence. Journaling allowed me to keep my painful secret while maintaining my sanity. I referred to these collective sheets written and ripped from a legal pad as "my journal." Luke repeatedly told me that no one would ever believe I was abused. I was a prosecutor, and I walked into the courthouse every day but never told anyone anything. Because of this, Luke said no one would believe an abuse allegation because there was no proof.

The stress was slathered on thick. Not only had Luke become mentally, physically and verbally abusive, he was also showing signs of being cunning and deceitful. When it came to checking the mailbox, Luke made sure he was there each and every time. I didn't think anything of it at the time, but I eventually found out he was only getting the mail because he wanted to intercept the bank statements of his secret bank account. Each semester he was in law school, he got about $10,000 in student loans for "living expenses." Without telling me, he put this money into a secret bank account, which allowed him to have his own spending money, so he didn't have to live according to the family budget.

He was also depositing some additional income into this separate account. When he was a police officer, he had been actively involved in the Harris County Deputies Organization and was the president at one point. He somehow got James, his best friend, to get the organization to pay him $1200 monthly for being a "consultant." He did absolutely *nothing* for this money and he and James joked about it. This was all during the time when he was not employed, which left me stressing about making ends meet on one income.

Around this time, Luke was putting an intense amount of stress on me to run for Sheriff of Harris County. The idea was completely ridiculous. A woman with no law enforcement experience would never be the elected Sheriff of the third-largest county in the United States. Luke insisted that it was a supervisory position and that my law degree was better than law enforcement experience. I disagreed, but he would not listen.

So, I set up a meeting with local party bigwigs, and they were able to convince Luke it was not a good idea. He listened to them. They suggested I run for District Court Judge instead. Luke jumped right on this, but I was not interested at all. I had enough stress with running my law practice and struggling to make ends meet financially. He continued to pressure me. He promised I would have the endorsement of the Harris County Deputies Organization, (which was a big deal) and that they would ensure I got other endorsements. I still can't believe he was able to pressure me into running for judge. The campaign would be lengthy and mentally and financially draining.

It was almost two years of non-stop campaigning, with an event on one side of Houston and then another event an hour away and on the other side of Houston, usually starting at the same time. I was expected to be at all events, but still, keep my practice up and running, while also being a good wife and mom. The pressure and cost of running a campaign were way more than I anticipated. I was also expected to make "contributions" to various local groups and events. As election night neared, I was emotionally and physically exhausted. I honestly didn't care if I won or lost, I just wanted it to end. Over the months during the campaign, the physical aspect of the abuse began to intensify.

7/18/2008

Yesterday I came in from work, walked in the bedroom and flipped on the light. I had no idea that Luke was sleeping. He freaked out and yelled at me that I had made too much noise this morning and he had not been able to get enough sleep. He started screaming, "What is something dear to you?" He looked around and grabbed my glasses and threw them against the wall. Then he came at me. I started backing up and he clawed at me in a desperate attempt to reach my neck. He wasn't able to grab to grab my neck, but he did manage to scratch me on my chest when he grabbed my necklace and ripped my necklace off. I ran out of the room, left and went to the mall. He called me wanting to know where I was because nothing happened to justify me running off. I was able to take a photograph of the scratch on my neck.

Where is the funny sweet man I fell in love with? I was so confused. My inner voice was giving me conflicting advice, sometimes it told me to run and other times, it told me that everything will be okay.

But, Why Did You Stay?

CHAPTER FIVE

What's In A Name?

Not long after we moved into the new house, Luke just had to have a new Corvette. I told him we couldn't afford it because I was the only one working, but he persisted and was relentless. He claimed it was a good investment because it would hold value. Our payments would be $1125 monthly, which I argued was absolutely insane and out of the question. But I finally relented when he said he would get a job and pay the note himself. I don't know how I qualified for this additional debt, but I was approved, and Luke got his Corvette. Luke did get a job as a deputy working for Precinct 2 Constable, but about two months after he began working there, Hurricane Ike hit. The department put everyone on mandatory overtime due to massive power outages and other issues. Despite my argument, this was a temporary situation, he insisted he couldn't handle the stress with law school.

8/14/2008

Luke quit his new job, complaining he could not handle all of the stress of working and going to school. I was upset because we had not discussed this and now, I would be the sole provider. He stormed out of the room and came back with his gun and said he was going to kill himself. I was sick of his drama and so I told him "fine, go ahead." He got very angry with me and grabbed me and tried to pull me into the bedroom. He slammed my head into the wall and slammed the door into my desk, damaging the door. He walked away and I shut the door. I was crying because my head hurt where he had slammed it in the wall. A few minutes later, through the closed door, I could hear Luke chamber a bullet into the gun. Luke said you're not going to help me and I need help. So, I opened the door, took the gun from him and dropped the clip out of the gun. We hugged and cried together. I told him we would make it through all of this. The stress is almost more than I can stand. If I don't win the election, I don't know how we are going to make it financially because I have turned away so many cases trying to be at political events. Even if I do get elected, I won't get my first check until February. The physical toll all this stress is taking on my body is unbelievable. I just want to wake up on Election Day.

10/9/2008

I caught Ryan playing video games when he was grounded and told him he knew he wasn't supposed to be playing them. Right then Luke appeared in the doorway, lunged toward Ryan and punched him in the head. Then Luke grabbed Ryan by the neck, picking him up and then slammed him down to the ground. I tried to get to Ryan, but he was already on the floor. Aside from discipline, Luke has never hurt Ryan like this before. Luke left and I took pictures of the hand marks on Ryan's neck and where Luke punched him in the side of his head. If he does it again, I will call the police.

Finally, election night arrived. We organized a "watch party" at a downtown restaurant, that we hoped would become a "victory party." Even Maile flew in to attend. When the early votes came out, I was way in the lead. But when all the votes were in, I lost by one percent. Luke examined the returns in the different precincts and concluded I lost because the white areas didn't vote for me because they thought I was black, based on my name. The newspaper actually ran a story on the candidates with ethnic sounding names who lost.

We were driving home with Mom and Maile in the car when Luke said, "Well, you have your mother to thank for the loss. If she hadn't given you a black person's name, you would be a judge right now."

This totally pissed me off. There was no recognition for all the work I put in for almost two years straight to do something I didn't even want to do. And yet he wanted to blame my mother for naming me Mekisha, a name that I grew to love and cherish.

When my mother was eight months pregnant with me, my parents still hadn't decided on my name. One evening, mom was watching an episode of *Gunsmoke*, which involved an Indian Princess, named Mekisha. Mom decided then that Mekisha would be my name. People always asked about the origin of my name. Mom had always told me my name was American Indian. It was not until recently that I found out about this *Gunsmoke* episode. Although I was teased in school, I came to love my name.

It's like Madonna – I don't have to even use my last name, and everyone knows who I am. The incessant teasing through school made me tough and gave me thick skin, which I use to this day.

I was convinced that if it had been meant for me to win, I would have, regardless of whether my name was Mekisha or Susan. I felt so bad for my mom and didn't want her to think my loss was in any way her fault. I was also embarrassed at my husband's rude remark and worried that Mom and Maile wouldn't like him after this remark. I found out later that none of my family or friends ever liked him. They merely tolerated him because he was my husband. Once the campaign was over, I thought things would get back to normal because there would be less stress, but Luke remained in a permanently bad mood.

2/16/2009

Last night was another bad night. We got in a fight because he was mad about me watching a recorded TV show. He wanted to have sex with me, but I told him that I did not feel like it because I was almost asleep. I told him to take his pillow and go sleep in the other bedroom and he did. I was going to the bathroom when he came pounding on the bedroom door. I was walking toward the door to open it up, when he kicked it open by breaking the door and ripping out the lock. I yelled at him that he was fucking stupid. I had barely said the word stupid when he punched me in my jaw. It hurt so bad. I jumped backwards onto the bed to get away from him, but he kept coming at me. He got on top of me and shoved my face into the bed. I was screaming, "My jaw, my jaw!" It hurt so badly. He would not get off me because he thought I was going to call the police. He reached over and took my work cell phone and my personal cell phone off the nightstand and turned them off. I promised him I would not call the police and reminded him that I never have all of the times in the past, which seemed to convince him and got off of me. There was blood on the sheet from my lip. I went into the bathroom and saw how swollen and bloody my lip was. Luke said he was sorry, but said that when I yelled at him, I set him off and he couldn't help how he reacted because he just snapped. He said that he did not even realize he had hit me until after he had. He said he was very sorry, but blamed it on me for yelling at him. I asked him if he was still going to hit me when I was pregnant, and he responded, "Of course not!" Then Luke insisted we "make love." I didn't want to, but he said I had to in order to prove I had forgiven him. He flipped me over and I cried into my pillow, but it didn't last long. I wonder sometimes if there will ever come a day when some prosecutor will be fighting to get these notes of my thoughts into evidence at my murder trial because Luke finally killed me. But I doubt it because if he kills me, he will kill himself as well. I know he'll do it again, so why do I stay? Am I like all the other women that I fought for as a prosecutor who needed help but weren't able to see it? Do I stay because I want a baby and I'm too old to start over? Do I stay because I really love Luke? Do I stay for Ryan?

In 2009, Ryan's Mom, Judy, signed a waiver terminating her parental rights to Ryan. I couldn't believe she actually signed it. I was so excited that I was actually going to be able to adopt Ryan. Judy was pregnant when she agreed to terminate her rights to Ryan. Years later, I found out that Luke forced her to sign the termination papers by threatening to enforce a back due child support order and telling her that if she refused, he would make sure she had her baby in a jail cell.

CHAPTER SIX

Call Me Jane

D espite all that was going on behind closed doors, Luke was determined to put up a united public front. Even though I had just lost my race for Judge, Luke wanted to move to a nearby county so he could run for political office. When I thought things couldn't get any worse, I felt blindsided and overwhelmed with the thought of another campaign and moving houses. We had just been through almost two years of campaign hell, and now he wanted to do it again? Luke decided we would lease out our current home and then move to a new house in the other county. We were already renting out our first home, so now we would have two rental properties to maintain.

In 2009, we moved into our new house and immediately Luke's campaign for public office began. Juggling Luke's campaign with work was extremely difficult. I immersed myself in the local Republican party to rally grass-roots support, by attending all the local Republican Women's groups and countless events.

When we moved, Luke asked me to change my name to Jane, because Mekisha was too ethnic sounding. Luke was running as a republican. The county was so overwhelmingly republican that no one even bothered running for democrat positions. God forbid someone hears he was married to "MEKISHA" and assume I was black.

Growing up, the family called me "Mekisha Jane" because I was so much like Grandma Jane. My mom didn't give me a middle name; it was just Mekisha. My Grandma Jane, her mother, didn't like this one bit. So, she volunteered to fill out school paperwork and listed my middle name as "Jane" and it stuck. There is a middle initial "J" printed on everything official, even my report cards (yes, I kept them).

I really didn't have a problem with adding Jane to my middle name because I saw it as a tribute to Grandma Jane. But telling people that my first name was Jane, rather than Mekisha, felt very weird. Mekisha had been my identity my whole life. When I introduced myself, it felt like I was talking about someone else. But I had learned over the years to pick my battles with Luke. Most times, it was easier to just agree with Luke. So, in an effort to avoid conflict, I agreed and legally added Jane to my name.

I was already an established attorney, known as Mekisha. I had to change everything – my business cards, my website, and I even asked people who had known me as Mekisha for years to call me Jane. In Court, on numerous occasions, a Judge called me Mekisha and my confused client would look at me with a look of "Who is Mekisha?" It was a complete disaster.

When colleagues in Houston asked why I changed my name to Jane, I lied and said because my clients could never pronounce my name. What else could I say? That I was afraid my husband would beat me if I didn't comply? I didn't want to admit this to myself, let alone anyone else. Years later, friends told me this should have triggered them to realize what was happening to me because I had always been so proud of my name and for me to agree to change it, there must have been something wrong.

5/15/2009

We drove over to the old house to get Christmas decorations out of the attic. Our neighbor Doug was outside tossing a ball with his kids when he came up and started talking with Luke and I. Luke walked away and went inside and I tried to shut down the conversation, but it took a minute. All of a sudden, we both heard the back-door slam extremely hard. I then told Doug I needed to go check on Luke to see if he needed help. Luke was mad because he did not have a flashlight and the bulb was out in the attic, so he couldn't see anything. I have no idea why he refused ask his neighbor of the past three years for a flashlight. We got in the car and down to the stop sign at the end of the street when Luke grabbed the sunglasses off the top of my head so hard that it pulled a big chunk of my hair out. I screamed and Ryan screamed also. He twisted and pulled until the lenses broke into pieces. He said that I should have ended the conversation with Doug sooner and came back inside to help him. I don't understand why he was so angry about me talking with our neighbor.

Luke finally graduated from law school on December 19, 2009. Because I was a graduate of the same law school, I was allowed to hood Luke in the hooding ceremony. A hooding ceremony happens during graduation and is where a dean or a faculty advisor places the doctoral hood on the graduate, signifying completion of the doctoral program. A photograph of us at graduation was featured in an article in the alumni magazine. I was thankful to have the stress of law school behind us and I hoped Luke would be happier now with his accomplishment.

During the next several months, I was so busy with Luke's campaign that I didn't have time to make journal entries. It was the same drama, day in and day out. However, by early January 2010, things were escalating, and I was getting more scared. But no one had a clue that I was being abused. I have chosen a few journal entries to share what I was experiencing during this time period.

1/8/2010

When I got home from court, Luke was lying in bed as usual. He was on his laptop and asked me who Dan, Chris, and David were. He saw that we all had become friends on Facebook. I explained that Maile used to date Dan and that we all used to be friends. He demanded to know who sent a friend request to whom. I got frustrated and told him he was being nosy and that he should be studying for the bar exam instead. He yelled, "FAT BITCH." Then he came charging at me in a rage. I pleaded, "Please don't hurt me!" I could see in his eyes what was going to happen. He grabbed me and put his hand over my mouth and pushed it up higher so that he was blocking my airway through my nose and mouth at the same time. I could not breathe. He put his other hand on my neck and forced me down on the bed. Before my head hit the pillow, I was able to gasp some air. He was pulling my hair and choking me. He asked me if I was going to shut up now and I shook my head yes and so he took his hand off my mouth. He asked me if I wanted to die, I said no. He said he could kill both of us because he only lives for Ryan. He kept asking if there was someone else, and I kept assuring him there was not anyone else and that I had not done anything wrong, but he did not believe me. I assured him I loved him and would never leave him. He finally let me up and I ran as fast as I could to the front door. Just as I opened the door, Luke came behind me and pushed it closed. He started freaking out again and saying that I was going to call the police. I dropped to the ground in a fetal position and kept saying, "I'm sorry I'm so sorry!" I was down on the floor begging him to let me go to the bathroom and he finally did. I looked at myself in the bathroom mirror and there were no bruises, just redness! I sat there and cried then I laid down in bed and he laid down next to me and held me. I could not stop crying. He said he was so sorry, and he just freaked out. All I could think about was what would've happened if I had made it to the front door. Would I have told someone? Where was I going to run? Luke left a few minutes later and I was able to take photos.

1/21/2010

It was about 3:00 pm and we were lying in bed watching a recorded show. He kept going on and on about how stressful it was studying for the bar exam and campaigning. I told him he was going to fail the bar if he didn't study. He backhanded me across the face, knocking my earring clean off. He left and drove around. He came home a few minutes later and started checking my phones to see if I called or texted anyone. I was crouched in the corner of our room, shaking and afraid he was going to get mad again, but he didn't and said he was sorry.

2/7/2010

I heard the back door slam. I turned around and saw that Luke was in a horrible mood. He growled, "What are you cooking for dinner?" I told him "I am trying to figure that out, but I'm sure whatever I cook won't be good enough for you." He punched me in the side of the head and said, "Don't fucking talk to me like that!"

2/18/2010

Today was the worst of the "treatments" (as Luke calls them) and they are getting worse and more violent each time. Today I called Luke on my way home from court at about 12:30pm. He was in a horrible mood and said that he was having the worst day ever but wouldn't say what was wrong. I got home he was lying on the bed with his laptop open. I asked him what was going on, but he wouldn't respond. He was being a total dick, so I told him, "you're being a dick." I walked into the bathroom closet to take my suit off. He snapped and came charging at me. I was backing up when he slammed me into the lower wooden bar which had clothes hanging on it. He then turned me to the left and slammed me against the closet door and then slammed me down to the floor. I hit my right elbow and tailbone really hard as I went down. He got on top of me, straddled me and as he was choking me, he screamed, "I told you to leave me alone, why do you do this to me?" He moved his hands over my mouth and pressed down as hard as he could. Then he grabbed the pair of pantyhose that I'd just taken off, balled it up and shoved the whole thing in my mouth. Then he grabbed my head with both hands, one on each side, and screamed, "look at me!" Then he picked up my head and slammed it on the floor. The pain was indescribable. It felt like my brains were coming out the back of my head. He punched me on my ear which stung. He kept saying, "you do this to me and you're not even sorry!" I kept saying I was sorry, so he would let me up, but he kept telling me "no you're not sorry," every time I apologized. Finally, he got off of me and went to the bedroom. I was crying on the floor when he came back with his gun. I thought he was going to kill me, but he left the house with the gun and I then left also. He kept calling me over and over. I was sitting in a parking lot because I didn't know what to do. He then had James call me because I would not answer his calls. James told me, "He's sorry, he really messed up." As I talked to James, I realized that Luke had not told him everything, so I did. James told me that since Luke was so sorry, we could work this out. I had blood running down the side of my neck where he grabbed me so hard that my earring post stabbed me in the neck. James again told me that Luke was really sorry and that I should call him. Luke was still calling me non-stop. I finally answered and he said this time he realized how easily he could have caused my brain to bleed or could have crushed my larynx. He did seem really sorry. My back hurt so badly and I just wanted to lay in my bed, so I went home, like always. I think I might really leave if he does it again. I had an IUI treatment exactly one week ago. What if I was pregnant? He said he didn't think about that. Maybe he won't hurt me if I'm pregnant. Since we moved, he jokes that they don't file assault family member cases here like they do in Houston. I hope that's not true if he kills me.

3/8/2010

I really almost died this time. We got a chocolate lab puppy and she is absolutely adorable. But today, she literally chewed everything in the house, focusing on the most expensive and sentimental items. Luke got upset with my complaining. He snatched the puppy up by the neck, threw her like a softball into the car and drove away. I called him but he didn't answer. He came back a few minutes later and said that he dumped her off in another neighborhood. I asked him "What are you going to tell Ryan?" Luke screamed, "Shut your CUNT voice up!" He said, "I do not want to hear your cunt voice ever again! I wish you were dead!" He said this repeatedly as he came at me. He grabbed

---

But, Why Did You Stay?

my throat and squeezed to the point that I felt like I was going to pass out. He kept re-positioning his hands on my throat to get a better grip. I honestly believed this was the time I was going to die. He dragged me across the room by my hair and got his gun and handcuffs and started to handcuff me behind my back and then dropped them and went for his gun. He shoved me on the bed and racked the slide back on the gun, chambering a round and held it to my head. I shut my eyes and he screamed for me to look at him and asked me, "Do you want to die?" I said no and looked away in fear. He screamed, "Look at me!" I wouldn't and looked down again. Finally, he put the gun down and asked me if I was going to call the police. I said no. I knew it would be my word against his and he always had a way of making people believe anything he said. I knew that they would believe him. I know one day I'm going to end up dead. Two days ago, I bought a camera at an electronics store and I was going to try to conceal it in a floral arrangement, but when I got it home it was too big and too conspicuous, so I had to return it. Obviously, I do not stay for financial reasons. I told him if he did it again, I would leave him. I hope he believes me. I don't want to leave him; I just don't want him to hurt me anymore.

5/7/2010

Last night Luke and I got into a huge fight because I grounded Ryan and then caught him playing his video game.

65 | P a g e

I was trying to explain to Luke why I grounded Ryan. Luke screamed, "Shut up, you stupid bitch!" and told Ryan to go to bed. I told Luke that I did not want him to talk that way to me in front of Ryan. Luke was waiting on a call from a friend of his to go have some drinks at the bar. I told him, "Why don't you just leave now!" And he asked if I wanted him to leave and I said yes. He started running at me. I screamed you better not hurt me and shut and locked the bedroom door. He beat on the door a few times and said he just wanted his shoes. I asked him which ones and then all of a sudden, he kicked the door open. I ran to my side of the bed and crouched down in the corner. He told me, "you started this," and he finally left for the bar. I was surprised but thankful he didn't hit me this time.

5/21/2010

Luke went to the bar to drink with his friend, the County Judge. I called him because the new renters had just called me and were needing things fixed. So I wanted to let him know what was happening. He returned my call on his way home. I could tell that he was drunk, and he said that he was going over there to tell the renters to "get the fuck out of his house and move back to where ever they came from in Asia." I told him this was not the kind of help that I needed and hung up. He pulled in the driveway, as I was leaving through the back door with a book to go to read at Starbucks. He got out of the car with his gun in his hand, put his arm around my neck and shoved the gun into my ear, pulling me back inside the house. Once inside, I ran out the front door and around to my car. I jumped in the car, locked the door and drove away just in time. I drove to a movie theater parking lot where I called him several times, but he did not answer. I called Ryan and asked him if Luke was home and he said no, so I started heading back to the house. Luke finally answered and said he was going to kill himself, but first he was going to call Ryan to tell him it was my fault. I immediately called Ryan and told him that if his dad called, he was not to answer the phone under any circumstances or listen to any voicemails. I told him I would be home in just a minute. I did not want this kind of stress put on Ryan. I got home and I listened to the voicemail and he was very sweet and told Ryan that he loved him dearly and always would. I went into the bedroom and found out that he crushed my camera and kicked a hole in the door. He ended up coming back home but told me that he withdrew $200 from the checking and rented a room inside the city of Houston. He always said he wanted to kill himself in Houston city limits, so that none of his co-workers would work his suicide scene. He told me it was as close as he has ever come to actually doing it. He hasn't even started studying for the bar exam, so I anticipate the stress level going way up.

5/23/2010

Ryan had been getting in trouble for taking food up to his room after we found half eaten corn dogs and pizza shoved under his dresser and cereal bowls full of moldy milk in his closet. I unloaded the dishwasher and told Luke we were low on bowls. I was in the bedroom when I heard screaming. I came out to find Luke on the stairs, holding Ryan's head up by his hair, and screaming, "Is this what you wanted?" I screamed at Luke, "You better fucking let him go now!" He did and left to get fast food. Ryan told me that Luke slammed his head on the stairs leaving an instant knot that was turning blue. I was able to take pictures when Luke was gone.

6/1/2010

I came out of the bathroom to get in bed for the night. Luke was packing a suitcase and I said, "What are you doing?" And he said that he had a conference tomorrow in Austin, and I asked him why he couldn't just leave in the morning. I didn't understand why he was making a decision to leave so late without having ever told me he had to go to a conference to begin with. He freaked out and broke my hairdryer and brush again. So, I told him I was sorry and that it was fine if he left. I had to go to Walmart to buy another hairdryer. I went into the closet to get dressed. He snatched my dress from my hands and started ripping it apart. I asked, "Why are you doing this?" He glared and said, "because you fucking deserve it." He reared back his fist as if he was going to hit me again, so I dropped to the floor and begged him not to. He told me to get into the bed and "act right." I ran to the bed and he did his usual thing asking me "Why I did this?" and "Why do I make these things happen?" He finally calmed down and allowed me go to Walmart for a new hair dryer.

I found myself engulfed in his world of turmoil and drama. He used his childhood trauma and his mother's death to spin himself into the victim in every situation. During one argument, Luke said he was going to kill me because he didn't want to ever see me with another man. I remember negotiating with him saying that instead of killing me, he could slice my face and leave a scar, so no man would want me. I was trying to stay alive. I was learning that Luke had demons he wasn't willing to face, which left him in denial of his violent characteristics and behaviors. I felt trapped, but I still believed I could make things better and make our marriage loving. So, I kept trying.

But, Why Did You Stay?

CHAPTER SEVEN

Lost In A Whirlwind of Trauma

I mistakenly assumed I could still have relationships with family and friends. Luke made it his mission to isolate me from everyone and he made it very clear that he didn't want to be around friends or family. In June of 2010, Layla, Katie and I planned a sister trip to see the Dixie Chicks, in concert in St. Louis. We love the Dixie Chicks and they have one song in particular that I connected with. "Goodbye Earl!" is about an abused girl and her best friend, who after years of abuse, came up with a plan to poison the abusive Earl, bury his body and live happily ever after. Whenever this song came on the radio, I belted the lyrics out, fantasizing what life would be like for me if Luke really were dead. Although I would never have the courage to act on these fantasies, it was still liberating to sing along to the song.

We didn't plan to be away from our families for long, just two days. Our flight left on a Saturday morning, the concert was Saturday night, and we would fly back the next morning. Luke agreed that I could go, but as the date approached, he kept telling me to cancel the trip and stay home with him. He was convinced that I would find someone else and sleep with them in their hotel room. These warped negative emotions were constant and exhausting.

God knows I needed this trip! I just needed some time to breathe without him hovering over me. I tried my best to ease his fears by explaining that all three of us would be in the same hotel room and nothing was going to happen. He finally agreed to let me go. I couldn't wait to unwind and enjoy the change in atmosphere.

Unfortunately, the peace I was hoping to experience during the trip didn't happen. Luke texted and called me constantly during the entire time I was gone. We barely made it to the hotel with just enough time to change clothes and grab a bite to eat downstairs before walking to the concert. I had already spoken to Luke several times that day, but he kept calling wanting to know what I was doing. When we finally got to the concert, I told him that I couldn't talk anymore because it was too loud for me to hear him. So, he switched to incessant texting. If I didn't reply to his text right away, he would send fifteen more.

All I wanted to do was sing along to the music and be there with my sisters, but he would not let that happen. When we got back to the hotel room, I called to tell him good night. He refused to believe I was in the hotel room with my sisters. To calm him down, I took pictures of them sleeping next to me and sent it as proof that we were all in the same room. After that, he finally let me go to sleep. He didn't text much the next day when we were on our way back, so I assumed he was over it. Despite the drama with him, I had a wonderful time with my sisters.

I got home to find Luke in one of his sour moods. When I walked in and put my luggage down, Luke told me it was wrong for me to go on trips without him. When I didn't respond with agreement he flew into a rage, slamming me down to the tile floor in the kitchen. My head bounced off the tile floor like a dodge ball hitting the wall in PE class. I initially thought my skull was cracked open. I felt the back of my head and, to my surprise, there was no blood; however, the impact instantly caused a tennis ball-sized knot. As I lay on the floor in pain, he kicked me in the stomach and told me to get up. I did everything within my power to comply, but not quickly enough. Again, he kicked me in my stomach, like I was a dog in the street.

As the tears streamed down my face, all I could think of was survival. Why was he doing this? Why wasn't he happy to see me? I was his wife, the woman he promised to cherish through sickness and health until death do us part. I was starting to feel dead inside. The longer I stayed in the relationship, the more he took from me. The more I tried to cover up for him, the more of myself I lost. I didn't know who I was anymore. I was allowing this man who once appeared to be a "knight in shining armor" to taint the bubbly, upbeat person that I had always been. I had prosecuted domestic violence cases but never imagined myself being on the other side. I defended the defenseless, but now I was defenseless. Who was going to save me?

7/19/2010

I woke up around midnight with Luke standing over me and holding a shotgun and saying that he was going to kill someone so he can get a Wikipedia page. He was talking about killing his political opponent or famous people; saying I would be able to write a book when he's finished. Then he grabbed his gun and walked out the back door and left. I had already taken my sleeping pill and was barely processing what was happening. I grabbed my keys and jumped in the car, following him with the hopes of preventing him from killing his political opponent or doing whatever he had planned. I was in a short nightgown with no underwear or shoes. I called James and told him what was going on. I turned out of our subdivision and did not see Luke's tail lights, so I had no idea which way he went. James told me where the political opponent lived, and so I drove over there to make sure Luke was not making good on his threats. James and I had agreed to work together in secret to try to keep him from doing crazy things. Our agreement was whenever we spoke on the phone, I would delete the call log and any messages. James got in touch with Luke and told me he was back home. James said he was calmed down. So, I went home. We both got back into bed and went to sleep. Around 2:00am, I heard a door slam and realized that Luke was not next to me. I found him sitting at the dining room table with his gun. I sat down at the table with him and saw a suicide note that he had written to Ryan. He said that he wanted to kill himself and that he's been wanting to kill himself for a long time. I sat at the table all night with him trying to convince him that things will get better. He told me that he would not want Ryan to live without him. Basically, saying that if he kills himself, he's going to kill Ryan also. I know if I ever left him, he would kill me. This is not how I thought my life would end up. I don't know what to do.

As much as I hoped and prayed for things to get better, they grew worse. One day I woke up from a nap in a puddle of dark red blood. I assumed I started my period. I got cleaned up and threw the sheets in the washer. I had to get my suitcase packed.

I was going to stay with Luke at the Hilton Downtown, where he was scheduled to take his 3-day bar exam the following morning. Luke said that I had to stay there with him at the hotel. I honestly have no clue why he insisted on me going. When I took the bar exam, I also stayed in a hotel to avoid driving before the exam. However, I didn't want another human anywhere near me.

Unfortunately, Luke was a different breed, like a dog with separation anxiety. He needed me to be there. I didn't say anything about the bleeding to him, but as I was packing, the blood continued to gush out of me. I started to get concerned because I had never seen that much blood before. I sat on the toilet and more came out. I assumed that this was a buildup of having had light periods. I dismissed my concern and continued packing.

I finished packing my bag and then packed all my work files for the week, but the blood wasn't stopping. It was a constant flow, which now had me concerned. I put a folded towel between my legs and sat down to think. Layla is in the medical field, so I called her. She insisted that I go to the emergency room, but I didn't have time for that. Luke had to take his exam and I wasn't about to interfere with that because my period was heavy. My focus was on Luke and helping him get through the bar exam. I needed him to pass so the stress level would go down. I didn't want to be the reason that he didn't pass or the reason he missed taking the exam. I tried to convince myself that I was fine.

Layla called Mom, who came right over. When my mother arrived and saw all the blood, she told me she was taking me to the hospital. I knew I needed to go, but I didn't want to. Luke was acting like himself, as if what I was experiencing wasn't a big deal. I reluctantly got in the car with Mom and she rushed me to the hospital. After arriving and getting checked by the doctor, I found out I was between two and three months pregnant and was having a miscarriage. I was devastated!

Luke and I had spent so much money on fertility treatments without success that I had pretty much given up on the idea of getting pregnant. But then, I conceived only to lose our child? Why? Why was this happening to me? All I wanted was to have a baby. Now, this opportunity had been snatched away. Quite naturally, I started playing back recent events and the argument we had the day before. Could that argument have caused me to lose our baby? Was it something I did or didn't do? There were so many thoughts rumbling through my mind. My emotions were running rampant, all over the place, and he wasn't even with me to hear this news.

Losing the baby was hard, but I wasn't far from losing my own life. According to the doctor, I lost over half the blood in my body and required a blood transfusion. To think if I had not called my sister, I could have died. I could have bled to death because I was so focused on Luke and his bar exam. In addition to the blood transfusion, I required immediate surgery to remove the remainder of the pregnancy and to stop the bleeding. This was a devastating blow that I was not expecting.

Right before the nurses wheeled me up to surgery, Luke finally showed up. I can't honestly say what his reaction or emotions were, but I wanted him to stay focused on the exam.

I convinced him to still go downtown and get checked into the hotel and promised him that I would be there with him tomorrow as soon as I was released.

The baby I had longed for was now gone. Was it a boy or a girl? Would I be able to ever get pregnant again or was this my final opportunity?

I pushed all these feelings and emotions to the side, so I could support Luke during his exam. There was no way I could handle being blamed for losing our baby *and* for him failing the bar. I was strong until he left, and then I cried like a baby in the arms of my mother who stayed with me in the hospital.

As they wheeled me into the cold operating room, I experienced a myriad of emotions. I was scared I might not wake up. When I did, I was eager to know my chances of giving birth again. Everything went well with the surgery. My body was back intact, but my heart was hurting. Experiencing any type of loss is difficult, but losing my baby was especially hard because I had longed for one so badly.

I missed work that next morning because I was still in the hospital. To be honest, I could have taken the whole week off to lay around and process the loss of my baby, but we couldn't afford it. "No bees, no honey; no work, no money!" As much as I wanted to go home to my own bed, I had to get to the hotel to be there for Luke. After all I had experienced, I forced myself to get to the Hilton as promised, to ensure that he was doing okay and provide whatever he needed. I was determined to set aside what I was feeling to help him feel secure so that he could do well.

Despite my efforts, he failed the exam. And as expected, he had the audacity to blame me! He claimed he failed because I was in the hospital when in actuality he failed because he didn't study. He used the miscarriage to garner sympathy from his colleges and friends, which also helped explain him failing the bar exam. This was one of many narcissistic episodes yet to come during our marriage.

CHAPTER EIGHT

Almost Saved By Grace

It was late October 2010 and the last day of early voting. My period was late, so I took a pregnancy test early that morning and it came back positive. I was pregnant again! Despite the abuse, I was extremely excited to know that I was given another chance to bring a new life into the world. I was so elated by the news, but Luke was still sleeping. I decided not to wake him because I wanted him to be in a good mood when I told him. I left the house before 7 AM to work the voting poll for the morning rush, so I could pass out campaign cards to all the voters. By 8:30, I left the poll to go to court. I needed to get back in time to work the poll for the lunch rush and throughout the afternoon and evening.

When I got home from court to change clothes, Luke was still in bed. I had left the pregnancy test on the counter hoping he would see it and be just as excited as I was. But I was only met with the disappointment of him still being asleep and not working the polls like all the other candidates. When he did finally wake up and hear the news, he expressed very little emotion toward the fact that he was about to be a father again.Despite his lack of effort, he won the election and was sworn into office in 2011. I was so thankful that after all these years, we would again be a dual income family. I hoped he would be less stressed having achieved this great accomplishment.

Over the course of my pregnancy, Luke was not involved and didn't go to the appointments. He told me I would have an abortion if the baby had any defects. I had hoped that his new position would have helped his depression, by lifting up his self-esteem. I did notice he wasn't as violent and thought things seemed to be calming down just a little. My optimism was soon replaced with the reality that he had not changed.

1/13/2011

I had just gotten out of court for the morning and was checking my voicemails. There was a voicemail from the principal saying Ryan had been in a fight at school. I returned the call to the principal, leaving a message on his voicemail. Then I called Luke and as soon as he answered the phone, he screamed, "I am dealing with it" and hung up. I drove home and Luke was pulling in the driveway at the same time with Ryan. Come to find out, Ryan had received a citation from the school officer for Class C disorderly conduct, for the fight he had been in. My attempt to discuss the situation with Luke turned into a fight that lasted until 2 AM. Luke's solution was to remove Ryan from public school and put him in a private school. I told him that was not the answer and that Ryan needed to learn how to better respond to situations. This is when Luke said, "I asked the police officer if he knew who I was? And told him that I would call the county judge and have this contract pulled and he wouldn't have a job." I pointed out to Luke that throwing his weight around wasn't a good move and that could cause negative press. Luke looked at me and said, "We are getting a divorce and I'm moving my paycheck to another account." (We had only received 1 paycheck from his new job.) Luke left and went drinking with James. When he came back, I thought he would have calmed down, but he continued the argument. We were in the bedroom when he pushed the door closed and would not let me leave. He grabbed my arm, leaving a red mark. When I tried to push past him and get the door open, Luke kicked me in the stomach so hard that I peed on myself. I started to scream in pain and dropped to the floor. I was so worried about whether the baby felt any pain or if she was hurt. He stormed passed me and went into the living room and started watching TV like nothing had happened. I got dressed and left. I had no idea where I was going. I felt so scared and confused. Part of me wanted to go to the police, but then I thought of how I would get to work without him finding me and killing me. I could easily stay someplace where he couldn't find me but the issue of going to the courthouse remained. No matter what, he would always be able to find me. I sat in my car at a gas station parking lot before deciding to go watch a movie by myself. I looked on the internet and found a 10:55pm showing. After I got inside the movie, Luke began calling me repeatedly, over and over. I ignored the calls but then he started texting. Then, I got a text message that said, "Help!" I stepped outside and called him. He sounded disoriented and told me that he did not know where he was. I could hear that he was driving and told me he had taken a bunch of Xanax. He sounded really messed up. I told him to pull over and I would come find him. Then, he told me "never mind" because he found the freeway and knew where he was. I left the movie theater and when I got home, he was already in bed. He said he was sorry for kicking me in the stomach and that he didn't want to hurt the baby. I don't know how many pills he had taken, but he was really high. I walked into the bathroom to find my jewelry thrown all over the bathroom floor. I finally mustered up the courage to tell him I was sick of his shit and that I hated him. He started screaming at me about getting a divorce and I said, "Fine, I'll move on quicker than you and I will be just fine!" He interpreted that to mean I was already sleeping with someone else and started accusing me again. He grabbed my arm and threw me on the bed. He put his hand over my mouth with his fingers pushed up to my nose so that I couldn't breathe. I didn't even have the energy to fight back. He was screaming that Ryan was a "lost cause" and that he should kill Ryan when he kills himself. I told him I would stop him, and he said he would kill me too. He finally loosened his grip and got off me. I wished I had cameras in my house to prove what I was going through. I will never get the courage to tell anyone. I feel so alone.

4/9/2011

This was one of the worst attacks yet. I hadn't been sleeping well because I was seven months pregnant. I woke up past 1 AM and got up to go to the bathroom. I got back in bed and Luke was still watching TV. I don't know why, but I was feeling underneath my arm and felt a lump in my armpit. I told Luke I felt a lump. I thought he would understand since his mom died of cancer. He told me it was nothing and to go back to sleep. I was very concerned and I couldn't fall asleep because I couldn't stop thinking about how big the lump was. But as always, he didn't seem to care. I told him that I felt like I was all alone, even though he was right there next to me and I started to cry. Out of nowhere, he grabbed my hair and pulled me over to his side of the bed. When he turned me over, he said, "Why do you do this to me, you fucking bitch?" He spit in my face and told me, "You're going to die!" He punched me in the side of the head several times. Then he grabbed both my phones from the nightstand and threw them onto the bathroom floor. He pulled me towards the end of the bed and got on top of me and was sitting on my chest because my belly was too big for him to sit anywhere else. He pinned my arms down with his knees. He kept telling me that "I did this" and that it was my fault and that he was going to kill me and then himself. He hit me multiple times in the side of my head, and mouth. He reached down and twisted my nipple to the point I thought he was going to rip it off and when I screamed, he let go. Then he hit me again in the head and told me to shut up, so I did immediately.

Then he dragged me across the bed by my hair and while still holding on to me, he got out of bed and reached in the armoire. I was pulling backwards because I knew what he was getting, his gun. But he had a good hold on my hair, and I couldn't get away even though he was holding on to me with only one hand. He pointed the gun to my head and said, "Do you want to die?" I begged him to please stop, but he was convinced there was no coming back from what he had just done. He went on ranting and raving about killing me and how selfish I was. I begged and pleaded with him not to kill the baby. Finally, he said, "If I get up, will you stay still long enough to let me get dressed so I can leave the house and go kill myself." I agreed! He got up, he got dressed and left. I can't explain the emotions of pain, horror, anger and frustration I felt. I was carrying his baby and he had no regard whatsoever for me or her. It was all about him. He was the victim. I finally pulled myself together enough to get up to get my phones. I put them back together and prayed that they still worked. I had to wait for them to reboot. I do believe that if it hadn't taken so long for them to come back on, I would have called the police. While I was waiting, I grabbed our video camera out of a drawer and started recording myself explaining what happened so that if he came back and killed me, the police would find the video and know what happened. (The next morning, I took pictures). Once my phones rebooted, Luke was immediately calling. I didn't know what to do. I answered it. He asked if I called the police and I assured him I had not. He asked if I was going to and I told him no. He asked me if I wanted him to kill himself or if I wanted the baby to have a father. I told him I didn't want him to kill himself. He asked me if I wanted him to come home. I didn't know what to say and knew that he was going to come home eventually so I said yes, I do. Normally, when he would come back home after having been in some sort of altercation, he would check my phones to see if I had called anyone. For some reason, this time he didn't check. And for some reason this time, I decided to set my phone to record audio and set it in the top drawer of the nightstand. While the phone was recording, I made sure to repeat everything he had just done to me. I told him that I hoped, that if he had killed me, the neighbors would have heard the shot and called the police so maybe they could save the baby. I told him that he had no clue what it felt like to fear for your life. His rebuttal was I didn't know what it felt like to hurt the ones you love and that was hard for him. Luke was tired, so the conversation was over at that point. The next morning, we went on as usual and continued to act like nothing happened, until the next incident occurred.

I thought about leaving Luke day in and day out, but I knew he would find me and kill me. There were no ifs, ands, or buts about it. It was only by the grace of God that he hadn't killed me already. I never in a million years thought I would be this woman, a "victim" of domestic violence. The drama with Luke never seemed to end. Life was a roller coaster, constantly up and down. Mentally, he was like a squirrel in traffic. I honestly don't know how I survived as long as I did.

Not long after the prior incident, Luke had been really depressed, more than usual. Several days in a row I found him holding a gun to his head, saying he was going to kill himself. So, I decided to hide the guns from him, but I forgot the shotgun. When he found out his guns were missing, he pointed the shotgun at me and said, "If you do not give me my guns back, you won't live long enough to regret it." I was so scared, and I immediately showed him where I had hidden his guns.

Then a couple of days later, I got the bright idea to remove all the guns from the house. I called his friend James and explained how suicidal Luke had been recently and I told him I needed to get the guns out of the house. James met me in a parking lot where I gave him all of the guns, including the shotgun.

That night Luke came home around midnight so drunk he couldn't walk. We didn't talk until the next day. When I told Luke that I gave his guns to James, Luke told me I ruined his relationship with James, and he couldn't trust me anymore. Luke also told me I was no longer allowed to text or call James and that I had better have all his guns back by the next day. I did.

Not long after that, I babysat for Layla, so that she and her husband John could go to his high school reunion. Again, Luke, being his narcissistic territorial self, was mad that I was not at home. He called me repeatedly yelling at me and told me that he had taken $10,000 out of our account so that he could leave me. I immediately checked online to discover he had withdrawn $10,000, which was almost all the money in our account. He ended up putting it back the next day after I apologized.

In June 2011, when I was eight months pregnant, Luke announced we were moving again because we needed to be homeowners in the county where he was now an elected official. Moving in the Texas heat in the middle of summer is awful, but add to that a huge baby in your belly doing gymnastics and that's a big fat NO. I refused but Luke insisted, and as usual, I relented. He found the house he wanted, and we closed immediately.

Now we owned three houses, which meant three notes! We were still paying both house notes on the houses in Clear Lake. We couldn't find a tenant on the more expensive house, due to the expensive lease amount of $3000. Luke's solution was to just stop making payments. He didn't care about a foreclosure because that house was in my name only, not his. He insisted that because we had new cars and a new house, it didn't matter if our credit was bad. I didn't want to have a foreclosure on my background, but I also didn't want to deal with the stress of arguing with him. I had no idea how I'd come up with an extra $3000 a month to pay the note. I suggested we try selling the house. He immediately shot that down saying there were too many repairs needed and refused to pay for the repairs necessary to put it on the market. I did not have the energy to argue, so, we stopped making payments on the house.

Moving day was a week before my due date. I was huge at 8 1/2 months pregnant. The movers arrived Saturday morning, and after a walk-through, told us they would not be able to move our flat screen TVs because they were not in boxes. This severely upset Luke, and he went into the bedroom and refused to come back out. Luke told me to tell the movers to get out because we were not moving! I told him we had to move because we had already closed on the new house. Luke told me I could move to the new house alone, but he was going to stay put. I went back into the living room and gave the movers the go ahead and told them I would get someone to move the TVs.

Luke was furious and reiterated that he was not moving and that I was moving into our new house alone. I told him that I was calling my sister and brother-in-law to come over and help move the TVs, which made him even angrier. He told me that if I did, he would divorce me. I knew that he was angry and having some kind of anxiety attack, but I couldn't move the TVs alone. Of course, my sister and brother-in-law dropped their plans and came to help. When they got there, Luke retreated into our closet, laid down on the floor, and refused to come out. After the moving truck and TVs were loaded, everyone but Luke headed to the new house.

A few hours later, Luke showed up and started talking to my brother-in-law as if nothing happened. I was too stressed to deal with an argument, so I played along as if nothing happened, pretending that Luke wasn't acting completely bipolar and irrational just hours prior.

CHAPTER NINE

Amazing Grace

Growing Gracie in my belly for nine months was truly the highlight of my life. Ok, that's a lie – I was miserable the entire time. Nothing fit, including my shoes. She sucked all the energy out of me, and I was exhausted all the time, no matter how much I slept. I had accomplished many things, but nothing could compare to the gift of a baby. I loved being a mother to Ryan but having the opportunity to feel a baby kick and move inside of you is indescribable. I wondered what she would look like. How would her little nose look? Luke didn't care what I named her, which was perfect, because I wanted to name her anyway. At first, I chose Elizabeth Grace, to honor my Grandma Jane, who's middle name was Elizabeth. I ultimately decided I liked Grace Elizabeth better. And so, it would be.

Despite the abuse in my life, I was in a happy place. I felt like things were about to get so much better. I worked non-stop to get unpacked and settled into our new home. Mom, Layla, and Katie came over and helped me get the nursery painted and decorated.

My due date of July 8, 2011, came and went. Gracie showed no signs of coming out! I met my aunt for lunch, ran some errands and then got a pedicure before the big day. I was so large and was completely miserable. I heard that certain pressure points on your feet could induce labor. So, in addition to wanting my toes to look pretty for the delivery room, I had an ulterior motive for the pedicure.

I did not realize it at the time, but my phone had no signal inside the nail salon. I missed multiple calls and texts from Luke. As soon as I walked out, my phone rang. It was Mom explaining that Luke had called her worried that I had gone into labor because he couldn't get in touch with me. I immediately called Luke back, and he was so pissed. I tried explaining that I did not get his calls because of the signal issue, but he just hung up on me.

I was just down the road and got home a few minutes later to find the suitcase I packed for the hospital dumped out all over the floor. Luke was packing his clothes in my suitcase and told Ryan to pack all of his clothes as well. Luke accused me of being off somewhere having sex with someone. The thought of having sex with anyone when I was nine months pregnant and too large to fit through a door was absolutely disgusting. Plus, it was something that I simply would not do. But Luke did not believe me. He made me spread my legs, as he had on prior occasions of insecurity, and he stuck his fingers inside me, checking for any suspect discharge. I was too emotionally exhausted to object, so I let him check. This still didn't satisfy him, and he said he was still leaving me.

I wasn't even upset that he was leaving. My daughter would be born in a matter of days, and this was the last thing I needed. I didn't want to put any more stress on me or her. I wanted him to leave and take all his drama with him. I was so fed up that I told him he could take all the money in our account and leave.

He was shocked by my response and paced around the house before finally deciding that he wasn't leaving. I was flooded with disappointment because I thought that this time, he was actually going to leave me. It would be the perfect end to our relationship. I would have my Gracie, and she wouldn't be subject to Luke's violent fits and outbursts.

As I re-packed my hospital bag, I found myself puzzled, truly wondering why he didn't leave. He finally had a job and could support himself. If I was truly the problem and I caused him to be constantly depressed and to hurt me, wouldn't he want to get away from me? I had been nothing but loyal and submissive the entire relationship. I was emotionally drained and paralyzed by fear.

A week later, on July 15, 2011, I was finally scheduled to be induced. We arrived at the hospital at 5:30 AM. There were so many emotions; I couldn't dare put them into words. I think it was the fear of the unknown that was the most intimidating. I wasn't sure how much pain I would feel or what to expect. I prayed that today would be about the delivery and no other drama, but honestly, even I knew that was a lot to ask.

As the morning progressed, my sisters, Mom and Dad arrived. As a family tradition, parents and sisters are allowed in the birthing room, and in fact, are expected to be there. When it came time to push, Dad knew he was to position himself appropriately. By this time, Layla had six kids and Katie three! And we all had been there, together, for every birth. Some people may think it's weird to have all these people in the delivery room, but we are a close family and a new baby truly is a miracle.

I couldn't help but think about how I wanted to shield my daughter from everything I experienced before and after conception. I couldn't wait to hold her, to hear her first cry and to look into her beautiful eyes.

As the day progressed, Gracie's arrival seemed distant, like it was never going to happen. The doctor who did the epidural, after the third try, yelled, "I got it!" Well, he didn't. Only half of my body was numb! I was in SO much pain. I tried to tell the nurses, but they said I couldn't have any more medication. I was not expecting it to be pleasant, but damn!

Luke announced that he needed to know when "it" was going to happen because he could not be in the room or he would pass out! Are you FUCKING kidding me? This was the first I heard of this! I noticed the facial response from my family; they were all in disbelief. EVERYONE was always in the room, there was never any deviation from this rule. Luke also noticed their disbelief and quickly retreated to the cafeteria, where he began texting me that EVERYONE needed to leave the room except the doctor. Well, that was a BIG FAT NO!! I was scared, and I didn't want to be alone. Then he left the hospital to get food because the hospital food sucked. I was trying to respond to his texts between contractions. It was a total shit show. Why did I expect anything less?

And the texts kept coming. He wanted updates. I wanted to reply to him that he could get his ass back to the room if he wanted to know what was happening, but I didn't want to escalate the situation in the middle of my delivery. I had been in labor all day. By midnight, I was only dilated to a nine. The doctor said he would have to do a C-section!! What the actual fuck? I was not mentally prepared for this!

I FREAKED OUT!! The alarm on my heart rate monitor started beeping and so did Grace's heart alarm. I knew I would feel the doctor cut my belly open with a blade. I could feel everything on the right side of my body. My sisters and Mom went into the hallway with the doctor and when they came back inside, there was a consensus the C-section had to happen. I was hysterical. Mom went back in the hallway with the doctor who told her continued labor was not an option.

Mom asked him what would happen in the olden days? He replied that the both of us would probably die.

I had been continuing to respond to Luke's incessant texts. He said under NO circumstances would I agree to a C-section! I tried explaining the situation over text, but I was in pain and tired. Mom came back into the room and said I had to do the C-section. I knew I had to; I was just really scared. My fucking phone would not stop blowing up with texts from Luke. The doctor finally agreed to put me under and then cut me open quickly, so he could get Gracie out before any of the drugs reached her.

I was able to calm down a little, knowing I wouldn't feel the pain. Luke continued to text orders not to agree to a C-section. He wanted me back at work in two weeks, making money, but recovering from a C-section would take more than two weeks. Finally, one of my sisters took my phone, and I put up no resistance. I didn't see it or Luke until I woke up in recovery the next morning. As I was being wheeled down the hall to surgery, I was overcome with an intense fear that I was going to die, and Grace would be all alone without me. I have *never* been more afraid in my life.

Despite my fears, I woke up the next morning to a perfect baby girl. Gracie was absolutely beautiful. She was everything I imagined and more. The first time I laid eyes on her, I was in awe of what I created. I was experiencing a joy that I couldn't explain. Her name was symbolic of the grace that had been bestowed upon my life.

Luke was surprisingly helpful and attentive during my recovery at the hospital and after we got home. We had only been home a few days when he began pressuring me to go back to work. I was in so much pain from the C-section that I didn't even want to get out of bed to pee. How the hell would I go back to work? But I got a little better each day. The pain was in NO way gone after two weeks, but I began to realize the stitches weren't going to pull open, and I wasn't actually going to die from the pain. I relented and agreed to go back to work after just two weeks. I would only be gone for 3-4 hours a day and Mom would watch Gracie. I was thankful I wouldn't have to worry about her being in daycare.

The night before I went back to work, I rocked her to sleep and prayed I could make things better than what they had been. Luke had been so wonderful after Gracie's delivery, I thought maybe this was the change our relationship needed. But it was an illusion. The peace did not last long.

8/5/2011

The stress for Luke was mounting at work because of the dynamics with some of the employees not getting along. When he took office, he hired several of his friends, put them in positions with no prior experience and this caused major resentment within the ranks. He walked in the door from work in a horrible mood and went to bed. I poked my head in the bedroom and asked him if he wanted to be alone and he said yes. Later he came into the living room and asked what was for dinner. I made several suggestions and then he without speaking abruptly left the house and came back with food just for him. So, I ate a bowl of cereal and made a pizza for Ryan. I went and got in bed with Gracie and he left again. When he came back, he was in an even worse mood. As soon as he walked in the bedroom, he punched the TV. He yelled, "Stop fucking with me!" I said, "What did I do?" We literally had barely talked the entire day and yesterday everything was fine. He screamed, "If you don't stop fucking with me, I will tie you up, drown "her" and "then kill you, Ryan and myself by burning the house down." I was crying extremely hard. I didn't understand why he was so angry. I told him that I wanted to run away! He replied, "There is nowhere you can run that I won't find you!" I truly believed him. Then he asked me for some of my pain pills from the C-Section and I gave them to him. He took them with his Xanax and ambien pill and passed out. I wish I had someone to talk to. I feel so alone.

I was so happy to be Gracie's mom that I found myself saying hello to random people in the hallway, all day long, and this is so not the person that I used to be. I was happier than ever. But all my happiness was overshadowed by my fucked-up relationship with Luke.

He would constantly taunt me by saying that he was going to kill me one day and that it was just a matter of time. He repeatedly told me, "There will be no divorce. I will kill you first." I tried to reassure him that I would never divorce him, and he said, "Yes, I know you won't." He made sure to remind me that a piece of paper couldn't protect me, that he would always find me no matter what.

8/24/2011

Luke went out of town to Austin for a work conference. At 5:00 in the morning, he called me drunk, but I didn't hear the phone because I was asleep. I woke up to a text that read, "you suck." Then he texted at lunchtime, "I need you here!" I was driving home from court, so I called him. He said he wanted me to go home, get Gracie and drive to Austin. I told him I couldn't come because I had to work in the morning. He called an hour or so later saying that he was depressed and was going to kill himself and that I needed to fly up there. I got on the computer checking flight times, but told him I didn't think I could make the next flight. The next flight after that left at 7:30pm. He told me that was too late and said never mind. I was baffled he wanted me to fly up there with the baby and then fly home early in the morning for court. I tried to talk to him about what he was feeling. He continued to emphasize how depressed he was and said he didn't want to talk on the phone anymore. Then he asked what I would tell Gracie if he killed himself. I started crying and begged him not to do that. In an attempt to cheer him up and give him some hope, I texted a picture of Gracie peacefully sleeping. Luke texted me a picture of his gun laying on the bed in his hotel room. I thought he might actually do it this time. I didn't know if he wanted to kill himself, as much as he wanted to kill me. I don't want to die, but more than anything, I want my sweet baby to live. I was so tired of the emotional merry-go-round. I fell asleep watching a television show about husbands who kill their wives. After watching the stories of those women, I am truly grateful that I made it through the pregnancy alive.

9/8/2011

Luke came home from the bar, drunk as usual. Gracie was asleep in her swing. In a drunken stupor, Luke took her out of her swing and lifted her up. We had a low ceiling in the hallway and when he lifted her up, he hit her head on the ceiling. This really upset me and I snatched her away from Luke and called him a "drunk bastard." I knew I wasn't allowed to call him this because he actually was a bastard and hated to be called one. I went into the bedroom and locked the door. He kicked the door open and took Gracie from me and threw her on the bed. Gracie was crying. My heart was aching, and I was frantic because it was one thing to put his hands on me, but now he was crossing the line. I tried to get to Gracie, but he grabbed me and pinned me down on the bed. Luke got on top of me, put his forearm across my throat and pressed down. He kept screaming, "YOU'RE GOING TO DIE!" I couldn't breathe, but all I could think about was my baby. He finally lifted his arm off my throat and bent down and bit my cheek! The pain was unbearable. It felt like he had bitten a chunk out of my face, and there was blood gushing out. I later realized that the wetness I felt was just his saliva and the pain caused me to envision an injury that was not there. After Luke bit me on the cheek, he got up, picked up Gracie and grabbed his gun out of the nightstand. While holding Gracie, he put the gun to his head. My first thought was that I wanted him to just pull the trigger, but if he did kill himself, he could fall on top of Gracie. He kept saying that I wanted him to do it, but I was begging him not to. Ryan heard allthe screaming and ran into our bedroom and Luke quickly concealed the gun behind his back. He screamed at Luke to leave me alone. Selfishly, I wanted Ryan to stay because maybe if he was there, maybe Luke wouldn't do anything in his presence. Luke yelled at him, "Go to your room!" Ryan said, "What are you going to do kill her?" Luke said, "I'll kill everyone in this house and then myself!" Ryan started screaming, "So you're going to kill me?" I told Ryan that everything was okay and to just go take his shower. Ryan left and shut the door. Luke put Grace back down on the bed and took my phones and threw them on the bathroom floor, breaking both of them. He got his keys and the gun and was about to leave the house. He went by Ryan's room first because he was pissed off Ryan had taken up for me. Luke came back to our bedroom and told me that Ryan was not in his room and he couldn't find him. And then Luke left. I couldn't call Ryan because I didn't have a phone. Holding Grace, I ran to the front door and screamed Ryan's name, when I heard the back door open behind me. Ryan had been hiding in a shed in the backyard in his towel. Then I heard Ryan's phone ringing. It was Luke. "I'm going to kill myself," he said. I reassured him that Ryan was home and had not told anyone or called the police. He was saying horrible things and it was during the conversation that I thought to myself, I wish I had a way to record this. I got a handheld tape recorder, held it up to the phone and recorded *him saying, "I'm a danger to you— one day I'm going to killyou in a very slow and painful manner —I'm fucked up, I mean, it's dangerous, don't you understand that?" I told him that he bit my face and he replied, "I'm going to do more, I'm going bite your trachea!" "WHY?" I asked. "Because I'm fucking crazy. I'm primitive. I'm a wild animal and if you push me, I'll bite! Don't you understand the danger? You need to call the police." He continued, "I hate life. I hate to live, to breathe. I hate it. My mother didn't love me, my father didn't love me, I'm fucked up. You should never have looked at me" (referring to the night we met). I finally convinced him that the police or no one else had been called and that he could come home. I told him that I loved him. I knew he would come home anyway, so it was the safest thing for me to do. He came home and we went to sleep. I woke up the next morning and found a sticky note where he had written his "Last Will and Testament" at some point the night before which read, "I leave all to the County Animal Shelter." The bite mark on my cheek turned into a purple bruise, despite the ice I put on it. I covered the bruise with make up.*

My fear of Luke was intensifying. He had thrown Gracie, made threats toward the entire family, and he was genuinely more terrifying than ever before. The next day, after the bite incident, we were talking about what had happened the night before. Luke told me, "You're really lucky I didn't kill you and if you were smart, you'd kill me!"

You hear stories about people "blacking out" and not remembering the violent attack they committed. But Luke always remembered every detail, until it was no longer convenient to remember. I couldn't believe the outrageously violent situation that had become my life. How could my life possibly get this far out of control? I just wanted someone to love and spend my life with.

There was nothing I could do to help Luke. I had tried everything. But I also knew he wasn't going to let me escape. He was going to continue to do everything in his power to make my life a living hell. I loved my Gracie so much. I was tired of constantly living in fear and now I had to consider the life of my innocent baby. I just wanted her to grow up and live a happy life. We would never be free. I began to condemn myself for marrying this monster and having a baby with him.

One night, I was feeding Gracie a bottle when I looked into her eyes and wondered if I would live to see her take her first steps, get her first tooth, say her first word, attend pre-k, graduate from high school, get married and most of all have children of her own. As I held her, I prayed I lived long enough to experience these things. I loved being her mommy and hoped it would last forever.

CHAPTER TEN

My New Normal

As always, Luke was in a perpetually bad mood and stressed about work. I was under the impression that things would get better after he won the election. Boy was I WRONG! Luke went to work late morning and was home by mid-afternoon. He usually slept in, sometimes as late as 10:00 AM, got to the office late morning and then left for the day around lunchtime. Some days he opted not to go in at all. Yet, he was surprised when rumors started to swirl questioning his work ethic. By September 2011, the physical violence and verbal terror continued to escalate.

9/23/2011

I was cleaning the house when Gracie started crying. Luke offered to take her when he saw that I couldn't get her to calm down. He was trying to feed her, but she continued to cry. He gave her back to me and said "take this fucking kid." After finally getting Gracie to sleep, I asked Luke, "Why don't you ever call her by her name?" He said, "I ought to punch you in your face, you need it." He said, "If you don't stop pushing me, I am going to drown you in the bathtub. I am going to fill the tub with water and stick your fucking head in it." I apologized, even though I wasn't sorry. Then, Luke said he wanted to go to the hospital for his depression. I offered to go with him, but he then refused to go. He threatened to kill himself and said he would take everyone with him. I begged him not to harm Gracie or Ryan. He responded that it was cruel to leave a child in this world without a parent. I dropped to my knees and begged him not to do anything. He said Gracie would never know it was coming and to stop the drama because I was pissing him off. He left the house and I fell asleep. Hours later, I woke up to him standing over me, just standing there, staring at me. I was afraid, but I didn't make any sudden moves. Then he opened my nightstand drawer and took out a bottle of Vicodin. I had been to the dentist, but I never took the pills because my tooth stopped hurting. He opened the bottle of ten pills and dumped them in my hand. He told me to swallow all the pills. I refused. Then he pulled out a small gun from his pocket. In a panic, I quickly agreed, "Okay, okay I'll take them, just give me the water bottle." He said, "Don't worry, I won't kill you with this gun because it's just a twenty-two." He looked at the pills in my hand and said they weren't enough to kill me, so never mind. Then he got in bed and went to sleep as if nothing happened. I will never kill myself. Now I have to worry about him staging a suicide verses him killing me, to avoid suspicion. The only way I would ever swallow a hand-full of pills was if he threatened to kill Grace. But I could totally envision a situation where he told me that if I take the pills, he would spare Gracie. I would do anything for her and he knows it. I hate what my life has become. There is nothing I can do. No one can help me. I could only be free of him if I were *rich and had enough money to hide. But as long as I'm employed, he will find me and kill me. I hope he kills just me. I need to get life insurance and make Layla the beneficiary so she can use the money to raise Gracie. But if he made my death look like a suicide, would the policy even pay out? I am so exhausted. I don't know how to escape this mental death trap. I can't leave him. He will kill me. I can't run away because he will find me.*

I constantly feared the inevitable future would end with him killing me. So, I emailed Layla and told her if anything happened to me, I wanted her to be able to get the money in my bank accounts without a court order and before Luke got to it. In the email, I explained I was mailing her a signed blank check and gave her instructions on how to log into my checking account online, consolidate all the money into that checking account, and then cash the check at the bank. I emphasized she needed to get it before Luke did.

Life with Luke continued to be unpredictable and disappointing. He was never in a good mood about anything.

9/24/2011

Luke left out of town for a conference and was scheduled to be gone for a few days. This gave me time to breathe. Most days I woke up with the sole objective being just to get through the day alive. I went to a surveillance specialty store to buy a nanny cam for the bedroom. Ironically, the store clerk's name was Angel. I explained to him that I was an attorney and needed a camera for my client to help our case. I told him my client was being abused and that we needed to document it. I told him that my client's husband was a police officer and that I needed hard proof, or no one would believe her. Angel picked out a covert camera that was disguised as an alarm clock. Now I will have video and audio, possibly of my murder, which I feel is imminent. I'm not sure why it makes me feel better to document what is happening to me because I know I can never use it against him and remain alive. He would kill me. I also downloaded an app to record all my phone calls with Luke.

The violence was intensifying. I wanted to make sure the truth was fully known in the end. I reminded my sisters over the years about the journal at my office. If Luke did murder me, I wanted there to be proof to prosecute him and prayed all my documentation I saved would ensure a lengthy prison sentence. I wrote a note to Layla on the inside of the folder where I kept my journal and told her that I wished I could have told her all this when I was alive and that "I hope you never read this."

While at the DA's office, I worked hard prosecuting family violence cases. I was assigned to the family violence division, specializing in cases where the woman recanted or did not want to cooperate with the prosecution. I prosecuted these cases because it is wrong for a man to hit a woman, but I never understood how these women would stay with someone who hurt them, someone like Luke. Now I understand. I couldn't believe all of this was happening to me. I couldn't believe that *I* was a victim. Never in a million years would I have thought *I* would be in this situation. The guilt I felt for bringing Gracie into this world of violence was constant and overwhelming.

I knew that Luke would never get any better. He was getting worse every day. The episodes were becoming more violent and scarier every time. And now he wasn't just threatening me, but Ryan and Gracie also. He refused to get any help or take any bi-polar medicine. There was nothing I could do except pray that he only killed himself.

10/29/2011

He came after me again. He threatened to kill me. He charged toward me from across the bedroom and acted like he was about to punch me. I begged and pleaded with him not to. Thankfully he didn't hit me. Later that night we were in bed and he told me to make "her" be quiet. I was so worried that I took Gracie to Ryan and asked him to rock her to sleep. When I came back, Luke was telling me how he needed to go on a trip because he was depressed. I told him he could go on a trip and sleep with whoever he wants, if that will make him happy. He responded, "That's how you get punched, that's how you get killed, what would you think if your head was stabbed?" I continued to apologize over and over until finally he shifted the conversation to politics. He was upset with one of the judges and he said, "I believe you don't take stuff; you've got to have a disproportionate response." Then he said he wanted to kill that specific judge to get even for things that were happening politically. He described how he would shoot him with a deer rifle and make it look like a car accident on the section of the freeway where there were no cameras. He finally fell asleep. I was lying in bed and the movie "Enough" with Jennifer

Lopez came on TV. Watching her character in the movie gave me chills because my life was so similar. The most chilling part was how the daughter's name was Grace and they called her Gracie. I was so envious of how she physically fought off her abuser. I could never do anything like that and live to tell about it. In the movie, she had people she could confide in and to be honest with. I can't tell anyone because it would only put them as risk as well.

10/31/2011

Luke was in one of his moods and fed up with the politics of his job. He was talking about killing people. I asked him, "Who are you talking about killing?" He said, "prosecutors." I said, "Are you serious?" He said to get prosecutors to understand, he would "chop off one's head" or the child of a prosecutor. When I asked what he expected to accomplish by cutting a prosecutor's kid's head off, he said, "Fear!"

Pouring my emotions onto a piece of paper was not as cathartic as I had imagined. No one was there to dry the tears, or to help hide the bruises. I was having to bear this all alone. I couldn't even tell my mother, who was always there for me no matter what. It was a miserable way to live, but it was my reality. This was worse than living in prison. My only joy and reason for living became Gracie.

11/2/2011

Tonight Luke said some very scary things. I had just got in bed and was rubbing lotion on my hands, before going to sleep. Luke came over to my side of the bed and told me that he is going to move me to the top of his "kill list." He said that killing just himself would be a waste and that he thinks he should kill some other people. When I asked him why, he said, "Because it's kinda a balancing act, you don't have to know but there's always going to be the possibility that someone could have anger inside of them and could act upon it. Kinda like at school when those Columbine kids go over there and just start shooting people, kids have to know that if you fuck with people that they could snap and start killing people."

11/21/2011

Luke and I were arguing in the living room, and I blurted out how much I hated my life. Big mistake! Before I could even blink his hands were around my neck and he was pushing me down to the ground and choking me. I screamed "let me go" until he finally did. I apologized, telling him I was just very tired and frustrated and battling fatigue from lack of sleep. I went into the bedroom and got in bed. He came charging in the room and got in my face and said, "Don't test me, I need to be sent to MHMR, there's a limit." (MHMR is a mental health facility that assesses and diagnose persons in mental crisis). Then he left and came back a minute later and grabbed my neck. He got in my face and said, "Do you want me to kill her?" I screamed, "No!" He said, "What did you fucking say to me?" and then he walked out of the bedroom. Later that night, he came to bed and pretended nothing happened.

11/25/2011

Gracie was very fussy and up way past her bedtime. I finally got her to sleep. Luke had been waiting for me to get her to sleep so we could watch TV together. I rocked her to sleep in her room and then I transferred her to the bassinet in our bedroom. Luke and I had decided once she was asleep, we would watch a recorded show together in the living room. Luke was on the bed looking on his laptop when I tried to get his attention without waking up the baby. He freaked out! He jumped out of bed and charged at me in a rage. I just knew he was going to hit me, but he didn't. He ordered me to leave the room with him and walked out. I sat on the bed and cried. He came back and again ordered me to come with him. I was scared, but I did it anyway. When we got in the living room, nothing else happened and we watched a recorded show. It's almost as if he knows there is a camera watching. Before getting the camera there was so much abuse taking place and now not as much. Not that I want him to hit me, it's just weird.

I daydreamed that if Luke ever divorced me, I would fight for custody and use my journal to prove he was an unfit father. Gracie was my baby. I knew he would try to take her from me out of spite and to avoid paying child support. He made so many past comments about how if he left me, I should give him all the money because I have the ability to make more and he doesn't. This was a ludicrous statement because he was an elected official with a more than decent salary to show for it. Everything with him was about money. When Gracie was first born, he talked about selling her for a million dollars because she was so perfect. I asked him, "Would you really do that?" He replied in a serious tone, "We could always have another baby." Just sick!

In late November of 2011, I used an ink pad to put my thumbprints on every page of my journal, in case he did kill me. My intent was to prevent a prosecutor from having to prove my handwriting during my murder trial. I was doing everything I could do to protect myself, but more importantly, to protect the truth. If I did tell someone, he'd likely kill me before I could leave him. I felt totally screwed and stuck in the nightmare that had become my life.

The physical and mental abuse had become so bad; I expected it. This was my new normal. Nothing made sense anymore. I became numb, living off of daily routine, for which I wasn't mentally or emotionally present. For lack of a better word, I was dead on the inside. The fear of how and when to get away was all-consuming. My mind was flooded with these thoughts of escape, but my desire to stay alive on a daily basis overpowered all other thoughts. Luke knew that I was paralyzed, and he enjoyed every minute of it. My only goal became staying alive for Gracie. I knew I had to leave him but figuring out a plan was complicated and overwhelming. Most days, I was too emotionally drained to even think about it.

CHAPTER ELEVEN

Willing Participant

I t was December 7, 2011, and although the holiday season had arrived, it didn't bring happiness, only continued abuse and drama. Luke was mad at me because he wanted me to attend a Christmas Party with him in downtown Houston. I was busy trying to finish a grand jury packet, which had to be delivered to the prosecutor in the morning and I completely forgot about the party. I had actually taken the case as a favor to Luke. One of Luke's cop friends needed help with a felony case for his wife's little brother.

Angry I had forgotten about the party, Luke spiraled into one of his childish rages. He grabbed my laptop and ran into the backyard, acting like he was going to throw it into the ditch behind our house. I begged him not to, reminding him that all my work and our family photos were on the laptop.

Ryan heard the commotion and came outside and screamed at Luke not to throw it. Luke glared at Ryan and followed him into his bedroom, demanding to know why he screamed. Ryan said, "Because it was stupid for you to throw the laptop over the fence."

Luke screamed, "You are a child, and you need to learn your place." In actuality, I believe Luke was upset because Ryan took my side. Luke screamed at his 13-year-old son to "pack his shit" and leave, and told Ryan, "You've just ruined our relationship, and I was the only person who loved you. You are never going to amount to anything without me. You better learn to work with your hands because that is all you would ever do." He continued yelling, "Why don't you go and find your mommy! Better yet, I'm driving you to CPS because I can't raise you anymore. So, pack your shit! You're hitting the road and everything in this room belongs to me!"

Luke then demanded that Ryan turn over his phone. As soon as Ryan gave it to him, Luke threw it on the floor. Every time I attempted to interject, Luke stopped yelling at Ryan long enough to yell at me, "Shut the fuck up," and then continued yelling at Ryan. I felt so sorry for him. Ryan told Luke that he was waiting for him to leave the room so he could pack. Luke told Ryan he wasn't leaving the room and "do it now."

Ryan opened a drawer, paused, and then slammed it shut and calmly replied, "You know what, I don't even need anything, I'm ready to go!" Luke yelled, "Fine, just go then!"

I stopped Ryan and told Luke he wasn't leaving. I told Ryan to go into the living room. Against my better judgment of knowing how Luke acted when I intervened, I begged Luke to apologize to Ryan. Instead, Luke stormed off into our bedroom. I heard the shower running and assumed he was getting ready to go to the Christmas party. I told Ryan to just calm down because Luke was about to leave.

A few minutes later, we heard the front door slam shut. Moments later my phone rang, and it was Luke. He yelled, "Everything that just happened was your fault; you constantly cause me problems." I pleaded with him that I was sorry. He was upset about having to go by himself. He asked if Ryan said anything after he left, and I said no. Then he again told me he was mad that I was working on this case. I reminded him that the only reason I was working on the case was as a favor to him. He told me that he wanted me to leave. I was thinking about where I was going to go.

Then he asked me if I wanted him to come home tonight. My mind was spinning. I started to answer, but before I could say anything, he immediately cut me off and said that I really didn't care about him at all. He again asked me if I was going to leave. I told him I would, but that I would rather leave on the weekend because I had so much stuff to pack up for Gracie and I had to work early in the morning.

He started in again complaining about me not getting ready for the party, and I told him that I would get ready right then and come meet him. He said it was too late. Then he started asking me about Ryan again said that he and Ryan would never be the same after tonight. Luke said that Ryan was "Fucked up" and that "He didn't have a shot in life."

Then he said, "So, obviously you're not going to your Christmas party tomorrow night since you fucked up my night tonight." He was referring to the annual Harris County Criminal Lawyers Association (HCCLA) Christmas party. I paid money to sponsor the party and was looking forward to going, but I agreed with him and said, "You're right, I'm not gonna go." He made me promise that I wasn't going to go.

Then he again told me he wanted a divorce and claimed he would file the papers in the morning. He then turned around and asked, "Is that what you want?" I was mentally and physically exhausted and still nowhere close to finishing the grand jury packet. I wanted him to just do whatever in the hell he was going to do, so I could move on.

I reminded him that things had not been good for a long time, and I didn't want Gracie to grow up in the middle of our dysfunction. I said, "Look at what happened today. She doesn't need to see or experience what Ryan did today."

Then he asked if I was going to take Ryan when I left. I said, "Well if you don't want him, I do." He said, "Yeah, I don't want him! I don't have any use for him or the way he acts." He kept me on the phone for over 20 minutes and only let me go when Gracie was screaming for a bottle.

I was in my study trying to finish the grand jury presentation when I heard someone walking down the hall. It was Luke. I turned around and stood up when he walked toward me. He raised the gun in his hand and put it directly to my forehead, touching me with it. Tears streamed down my face, and I shook with fear. I covered my face and dropped to my knees and begged him not to kill me. He lowered the gun and sat down in my chair. He kept repeating, "Why did you do this to me; it's all your fault!" I sat quietly, afraid to respond.

He continued, "So, you are the victim?" I replied with the answer he wanted, "no." He said, "Good because the first time you were a victim, but every other time you've been a willing participant; do you understand that?"

Reluctantly, I responded, "yes." He got up, took his gun and left the house again.

CHAPTER TWELVE

What's Love Got To Do With It?

I have to admit his "willing participant" remark and awareness of what my life had become caused me to question myself even more. It felt as if he was confessing that after all this time, he had been making my life a living hell only because I allowed it. If I had stood up to him after the first time, would we be in a better place?

I continued to work on the grand jury packet, and everything was quiet for a couple of hours. I began to worry that if I didn't call him and try to fix the situation, he would come home even angrier. I was petrified thinking of the repercussions once he got home. So, I called him. He answered the phone and screamed, "What?!"

I said, "I was just calling to check on you."

He replied, "Why? You don't care about me!"

I said, "Luke, I do love you. Are you really going to divorce me?"

He replied, "NO, I'M GOING TO KILL YOU!"

Again, begging and pleading I said, "Why are you going to kill me?"

He said, "Because of fucking who you are to me! Life disappoints me, and you are a part of that!"

I reminded him that after one of our past arguments, he previously promised that he would never kill me. He responded, "Oh well, I lied!"

A little while later, he called and asked what I was doing. I told him I was still working on the grand jury presentation. I just wanted to be left alone to finish without interference. Between the calls and worrying about his next move, I couldn't focus.

Again, he said he was going to file for divorce. When I asked if he was really going to do it, he responded, "EITHER I DIVORCE YOU OR FUCKING KILL EVERYONE, ONE OF THE TWO." I pleaded, "Please don't do this Luke. I thought you loved me."

He said, "Love has NOTHING to do with it. I can love you and fucking slaughter you at the same time. Don't you understand that?"

He then told him he was going to a bar and hung up. As hard as it was, I finished the presentation and got ready for bed. Luke came home in the wee hours of the morning very drunk and fell into bed.

When I left the next morning, Luke was still asleep. He called me around lunchtime, not long after I walked out of the courthouse. He asked me how my day went. To continue the conversation, I asked what was going on with him. He said, "Oh nothing, just trying to get this divorce filed."

I said, "Well, I didn't know if you'd feel differently today."

He said, "No, it is what it is." I told him he could have whatever he wanted in the divorce, referring to items in the house.

He said, "I am a time bomb waiting to explode, and I need to be by myself. You have no idea what is about to happen, and you don't want to be caught in the middle of what's gonna happen. But there is nothing anyone can do to change it."

The realization of these words of prediction was beyond my comprehension at the time. I told him I loved him, and he said he would see me later and hung up. He came home later and acted like nothing had happened and said we were going to the HCCLA Christmas party. This Jekyll and Hyde behavior was par for the course and not surprising.

In chapter 1, I left off explaining what happened prior to my arrival at the hospital. I was convinced that I was going to die. After being at the hospital for a while, I learned I was not that critical. The ER personnel were actually paying very little attention to me, as there were more serious cases coming into the emergency room. They cut my dress off my body, and I laid on the cold table for what seemed like an eternity.

The police officers wanted to interview me, but I did not want to talk to them. I told them that I was in too much pain to think and said that I would not talk to them until I got pain medicine. Needless to say, they were not pleased. I could tell they didn't want to be there.

Luke sent James to the hospital. James arrived at my bedside before the pain medicine did. I knew Luke sent him for damage control and to find out what exactly what was transpiring. James was still next to me when the police officers returned to the room wanting me to tell them what happened.

The officers asked me who James was and I told them that he was my husband's best friend, expecting that they would require him to leave. To my surprise, they did not after James told them he was a police officer. I really didn't want to talk to them, but I certainly wasn't going to say anything in front of James. I knew James would turn around and tell Luke everything I said. So, I told the officers that I had nothing to say. Even if James had not been there, I don't know that I would have been able to admit to the officers what had happened.

I was extremely afraid. The officers were clearly pissed I had wasted their time. They left the room only to be confronted by Cary, who rode in the ambulance with me, about not taking pictures of my head. Cary told them if they didn't take pictures, she would and then explain to their superiors how they had not done their job. The officers returned to my room, took pictures of my injuries, and left quickly.

There was discussion about possible facial reconstructive surgery. The doctors wanted to ensure I didn't have an occipital and/or facial fracture. We learned after the x-ray that I did not. My head was split open in a rainbow shape from the center of the forehead to above my left ear. My nose was broken, requiring stitches - two on the bridge of my nose and six above my lip underneath my nose.

I also needed nearly 100 stitches to close the gash on my forehead. They also used staples to hold the wound closed. Both my pinky fingers were broken. To this day, both fingers are crooked and will not lie flat. One doctor told me I was lucky he was working that night because his stitching skills were top notch. He was right.

Mom showed up at the hospital and when she told me she dropped Gracie at Layla's, my heart sank. I made her call Layla to make sure she had a gun ready. Mom stayed with me until I was released the next day. When it was finally time to leave, Mom went to get the car, and I waited for her to pick me up. I went into the bathroom and I looked at myself. I did not recognize who I was looking at. I knew it was me, but my mind struggled to register what I was seeing in the mirror. I just wanted to go to sleep and wake up from this horrible dream.

After leaving the hospital, I went to stay at my mother's house. Luke called very distraught and apologized profusely. He wanted to see me, but I told him I was staying with mom until we got counseling and then I would move back home. I had no intention of ever going back, but I was too scared to tell him.

While Luke was at work, my entire family came in multiple cars to help me get everything I needed out of the house. I knew anything I left behind would likely be destroyed. We loaded six cars up full of keepsakes, clothes, work files, and all of Gracie's stuff.

The next day Luke checked himself into the psych ward, where he stayed a few days. I think he thought that if he could tell people that he was sick, he could create some sort of sympathy and explanation for what happened.

A detective kept calling me, but I sent his calls to voicemail. I didn't want to deal with it. I was too overwhelmed. I had not yet finalized my plan to get out of the relationship. Minutes after the detective called, Jane Waters called me. She was the division chief of the family criminal law division at the district attorney's office. She had also been my supervisor when I was a prosecutor assigned to that division. When I saw her name come across the caller ID, I immediately sent the call to voicemail.

I knew what they wanted. They wanted me to give them enough information to make a solid case against Luke. The severity of my injuries caused the wheels of justice to turn without me wanting them to.

I knew what Luke wanted. He wanted me to make the impending criminal charges against him go away. He apologized and blamed what happened on his traumatic childhood. He promised he would get counseling and swore that nothing like this would ever happen again. I knew continued abuse was inevitable, but the thought of leaving him was scarier than everything I had already been through. He had told me over and over that, if I ever left him, he would kill me, and my family. I believed him. So, what could I do other than tell him I am not going to leave? I convinced Luke that I just needed some time to get over what happened.

But in reality, I knew this was *finally* my opportunity to leave. But I had to move slowly and methodically. Any quick movements would make him volatile. For almost a month, Luke came over to Mom's house to eat dinner with us almost every night. He thought that we were going to get back together after counseling, but I had no intention of ever being alone with him again. Before I broke the news to him that I was never coming back, I had to plan and prepare.

I took a few days off work and silenced my phone. Not just because my face was swollen and bruised, but because what I had feared for so long had now become a reality. EVERYONE in my professional community, including prosecutors, judges, and attorneys, all now knew my shameful secret.

When I finally did check my phone, it was filled with missed calls and messages. The Houston Police Department detective and Jane Waters from the District Attorney's Office had both left messages. I did not want to deal with the situation. I wanted it all to go away. The best coping mechanism I had was pretending everything is fine. But it was not working this time. I told Luke that Jane and the detective were calling and that I heard rumors Jane was planning on filing a felony assault, not a misdemeanor.

Luke was putting pressure on me to tell a version that wasn't true. He wanted me to say that **I** was the one who was drunk. When **I** tried to grab the steering wheel, he had no other choice but to push me off to maintain control of the vehicle and avoid a collision. So, my broken nose was an accident, with no intent necessary for the criminal charge of assault. Then he wanted me to say I just jumped out of the car because I was drunk, and he was not at all responsible for my drunken actions.

I thought about this rendition for a long time. I thought about what he was asking. If I told this version, I could still get divorced, but possibly keep myself from being labeled a victim. I had avoided the victim label at all costs and here it was, banging on my door. I didn't want to deal with people treating me differently. Plus, I didn't want him to get charged, for fear of making him even more unstable.

Despite the countless domestic violence cases I defended and won for my clients, I feared my reputation as a strong advocate and capable trial attorney in all types of criminal cases, including family violence cases, was in jeopardy. If I explained this was all an accident between two drunk people, it would be a totally believable story. I just wanted to be free from all the physical and verbal abuse.

Still dodging calls, five days after, I went to talk with Joe Bailey. I worked for his law firm during my third year in law school, and I knew Joe would help me decide what to do. I went into our visit thinking he was going to give me advice on how to minimize the exposure and how to maintain my reputation, by telling Luke's version of the event. I told him everything. He looked right at me and told me, "You have to tell the TRUTH." This is not what I wanted to hear, but I knew that I couldn't see as clearly as Joe, and I trusted him. I thanked him and left.

On my way home, I stopped by my office to grab some client files. I shared office space with several other attorneys and their staff. From behind the reception desk, my co-worker and friend, Catti, asked, "May I help you?" not recognizing me at all. I saw her almost every day, yet she didn't recognize me because of my injuries. When I spoke, she recognized my voice and began screaming and crying hysterically. We would talk about this moment for years to come.

CHAPTER THIRTEEN

Courage to Leave

My mind was replaying what Joe, my mentor, told me. While I was finally ready, to tell the truth, I was afraid of how my secret would damage my reputation professionally. I was humiliated by all the courthouse gossip amongst my colleagues. I viewed the violence as being half my fault. No matter how many times you hear it's not your fault, or how many times someone tells you that you did nothing wrong, it doesn't feel that way. What if I had left him the first time he ever hit me? Would he have realized he was wrong and not done it again? Did I perpetuate the violence by allowing it to happen over and over? Was this my fault? What would people think?

To help me come to terms with all of this, I needed to talk to Luke's first wife and Ryan's mom, Judy. I reached out to her, and thankfully she agreed to talk to me. She confirmed that she fled the relationship because Luke was violent. She was forced to leave Ryan behind because she knew it was the only way of making a clean break. Luke was not able to care for Ryan, so he left him with Judy's Aunt. Judy was able to visit Ryan that way. She told me that Luke was violent during the entire relationship. Her experiences with Luke were right on point with what I had experienced. It all lined up like a puzzle piece now. The epiphany that all the years of abuse he put me through, was ALL HIM and that none of it was MY fault, hit me hard. After Judy left Luke, and he realized she was not coming back, he went into attack mode. He told me that he asked his cop friends to pull her over and take her to jail for anything they could.

I found out that during this time, in June of 2000, Luke went to the family violence division of the district attorney's office and applied for a protective order *against* Judy. When the caseworker was talking with him, he admitted to begging her to stay with him just earlier that day. Judy had refused and he was clearly angry about that. He also told the caseworker that he would keep Judy from seeing Ryan. He further admitted to the caseworker, his plan to get charges filed on Judy by making a false report that she had threatened him and get that officer to file charges on her for terroristic threat. Luke also admitted to showing up at places where Judy was and going through her car and opening her mail. He left the DA's office furious that his protective order request was denied.

Ironically, after Luke's visit to the DA's office, Jane Waters wrote a letter to the police chief (where Luke was employed) explaining that Luke became very upset when the district attorney's office declined to seek a protective order on Judy. She further explained that in his mental state, she was concerned that he was a danger to his wife, child, himself and others. Although Luke complained about this letter in his personnel file for years to come, Jane's concerns certainly proved valid.

Jane and the detective were still calling me. Luke and I both knew this wasn't going to go away. He wanted me to get Jane to agree to only file a misdemeanor, rather than a felony assault. He also wanted me to write a letter saying that I didn't want a protective order. I wrote the letter with Luke standing over me one night at Mom's house. I talked to Jane about not filing the felony and she agreed, but only on the condition, Luke agreed to plead guilty to a misdemeanor assault deferred probation on the first court date. Luke agreed and a court date was set for December 27, 2011.

Although this sounds like a great outcome for Luke, it still carried many consequences for him. Luke was still a certified Texas Peace Officer, which would now be revoked by the state. He was an elected official with a law degree. His elected position would come under scrutiny and he could be denied a law license, even if he passed the bar exam.

Luke continued to come over to Mom's almost every day. It was killing my mom, but I told her it had to be this way until I felt safe enough to tell him I was leaving. My sisters saw me as a victim who couldn't get away from him. But I knew exactly what I was doing. It hurt that they didn't believe in me, but I didn't have time to think about those feelings. Luke thought that he could salvage our marriage if he accepted responsibility for what he had done. At this point, I had no intention of staying in the relationship, but I wanted him to publicly accept responsibility for all he had done to me.

Once the family violence charge was filed against Luke, the whole ordeal was intensely covered by the media in Houston and surrounding areas. Gossip circles amongst attorneys at the courthouse were running rampant. Luckily, I was able to take some time off because the courthouse is slow around Christmas.

In my family, my sisters and parents have always celebrated Christmas on Christmas Eve. I was so excited because it was Gracie's first Christmas, but the dark cloud of having to tell Luke we were getting a divorce was looming over me. I celebrated Christmas Eve with my family and thankfully Luke didn't want to come (because he knew everyone hated him). I only have one picture with Grace on that Christmas, and you can clearly see my two black eyes from my broken nose, three weeks after Luke punched me.

To maintain the pretense for Luke that everything was alright, on Christmas Day, I agreed to meet Luke and Ryan at James' house for a Christmas dinner. In an attempt to show the world that everything was fine, Luke posted a picture of all of us on Facebook. I felt nauseous listening to Luke speak and seeing him joking lightheartedly like he hadn't destroyed our lives. But I was able to get through the evening mentally because I knew I was going home alone.

On December 27, 2011, Luke pleaded guilty to Assault on a Family Member and accepted one-year deferred adjudication probation, with no jail time. I was present in the courtroom and anxiously awaited the part where the Judge said, "How do you plead, guilty or not?" When I heard Luke say "guilty," I felt vindicated for all the times he told me no one would believe me.

In the days following Christmas, Luke wanted to see me, but I made excuses, mostly that I had a migraine. But finally, I couldn't put it off anymore. It was New Year's Day; we were set to go to our first marriage counseling session the next day. There was no way I could sit through that, so I decided it was time. I made a copy of my journal and dropped it off on Luke's porch with a letter telling him that I wanted a divorce and that I was never going to come back home. I soon discovered that wanting to leave, trying to leave, being gone, and being free were very different.

The continued media coverage was humiliating, but one good thing did come of it. An old friend reached out that I had not talked to in years, Todd Trlicek. He and I first met when we waited tables together during high school. I was 16 and he was 18 years old. We never dated then because when we initially met, he was already engaged to another girl and had a baby on the way. We were just really good friends.

Todd was actually the person who introduced me to one of his best friends, Sean, who ended up being my first husband. Todd was the best man in my first wedding, and I attended his first wedding. We were good friends during high school, but I had not talked to him in years. Prior to him reaching out to me, we had not even been connected on social media. It was a genuine call to see how I was doing and if I needed anything. We talked about old times, and I thanked him for calling. I didn't talk to him again for a few months, finding out later that when he called to check on me, he had just been diagnosed with leukemia and had a lot going on himself.

After New Year's, I unfriended Luke on Facebook. He begged me to re-friend him in a desperate attempt to maintain the public perception that we were still friends. Reluctantly, I agreed, and I re-friended him.

Although Luke pleaded guilty to and was on probation for domestic violence, he somehow managed to convince his group of friends, even politically connected people, the entire isolated incident was blown out of proportion. He told everyone the lie version that he originally asked me to tell Jane and the detective.

His version of the events left him looking like a victim who was forced to plead guilty to something he didn't actually do. I grabbed the steering wheel, leaving him no choice but to push me, accidentally breaking my nose. I jumped out of the car.

I should have been shocked at his ability to spin the situation around where he was left as the victim, but I was not. The fact that so many people believed him after he pleaded guilty in open court was shocking, but this is exactly why I believed him when he threatened me, saying no one would believe me if I ever claimed he abused me.

Shortly thereafter, divorce proceedings began. I was still talking to Luke on the phone and recording all of our phone calls. (In Texas, it's legal to record a conversation, as long as one party to the conversation knows it's being recorded.) He relentlessly begged me to get back together with him, and even promised to get castrated if I would come home. One call from January 11, 2012, he rambled on:

"Do you still love me at all at least? Honestly? In your heart? You have to at least love me. I'm not saying being in love with me. I'm not saying you wanna be with me. I'm not saying that you wanna kiss me, but there has to be love because I don't understand. I looked in your eyes. I know that you loved me. I love you. It can't just go away.

You're crying. You must love me. I'm Gracie's father. She looks just like me. I've never cheated on you. I just crossed lines I shouldn't have crossed, boundaries. And that thing Katie sent, she's talking about those that don't let them go and new mornings and stuff like that, that made me cry so much because I've been like, I mean, it reinforces how bad I was and how I shouldn't have treated you the way I did and how I did it to somebody I loved more than anybody in the world and how I'm the one who's paying for it. The pain that I feel emotionally, the fact I can't sleep at night, that I've lost 27 pounds. I'm 180-something pounds. I haven't weighed this much since I was in high school. I don't eat. I'm, I'm, I'm heartbroken like more than when my mother died. So, I promise you I'm paying a heavy, heavy price, a heavy price.

You're the love of my life, Mekisha. You're the person who made me what I am except the bad. You've brought all the good out in me. I love you and always will and I'll follow your wishes because of that.

And then later in the same conversation, he told me, "If I were gonna harm you Mekisha, you'd be dead already. You know it and I know it. There's nothing anybody can do. If I wanted to kill you, I'd catch you when you were walking. If I was gonna kill you, you'd be dead. We'd both be dead if that's what I wanted. Please tell me you love Gracie's dad. Do you think there's a chance we can reconcile? I know what my problem was. I was controlling. I have super fucking control problems and the therapist is going over it with me. I hate myself for what I did. I'm so sorry. I'm really sorry. I'm without the woman that I love. The woman that I worship."

Trying to be very clear, I told him, "I don't love you. Each time you beat me, I loved you a little less, and now it's all gone. There's nothing left. You beat it all out of me."

I wanted to never talk to him again, but that was not possible. I still had to finalize the divorce and child custody issues. I had to remain civil with him in hopes of getting what I wanted: sole custody of Gracie. Luke told me that he didn't want to pay child support for eighteen years on a kid that I was "going to brainwash anyway," and he was willing to agree to the termination of his rights of Gracie in exchange for not having to pay child support. I was thrilled! This is all I ever wanted – to be free from him, his abuse and to raise my daughter in a loving environment.

By February, the tone of our conversations changed. Luke told me that he had talked to other elected officials and judges, who were telling him to fight for Gracie in the divorce. He was extremely concerned about public perception and didn't want people to find out he was agreeing to give up his rights to his own child. I made it clear to Luke that I didn't want to publicly air the private details of our relationship in open court, but that I would, to keep Gracie safe.

To intimidate me, he name-dropped various elected officials and Judges who had offered to help get his probation early terminated or help with the custody battle. He wanted to re-open his criminal case, alleging he was "forced" to plead guilty. He told me that because I had been "plotting" by keeping all this documentation over the years that I looked like a "deceptive individual." He said I would never win full custody and that no one would believe I was abused because I voluntarily went through fertility treatments.

Then, minutes later, he told me, *"I think you're beautiful. I love your green eyes, your pretty hair. I love the way you are. I love to snuggle with you. I love you so much. I'm not going to kill you. If I were, there's nothing you could do. But I'm not going to kill you; I love you."* It was a constant roller coaster.

On my birthday, March 24, 2012, he posted on my Facebook page "Happy Birthday." I did not click the "like" button on his post, but I did click the "like" button on other posts, specifically a happy birthday post from Todd Trlicek. When Luke saw this, it completely sent him over the edge. He called me in a rage saying I was wrong for skipping his post, then hung up on me. He then sent me a text that read, "Time is a precious thing that all of us have. Tick Tock. Free will." I called him to ask what this meant. He said I would never be safe. He begged me to have a warrant issued for his arrest. He said I had pushed him too far, and said, "I'm the only person that matters, judge and jury of one." He said he knew I was recording him and said I could play it all for the jury because he didn't fucking care. He warned, "If I decided to kill you, you wouldn't even know what happened. So, as I told you before, alarms and guns don't protect you." After hours of trying, I finally got him calmed down, and we planned to meet the next day to discuss divorce terms.

That night, my family hosted a huge 40th Birthday Party for me at Layla's house. My mind was racing. This would be the perfect opportunity for him to kill everyone that loved me because we would all be in one place. I seriously considered canceling the event, but I was trying to resume a normal life. I hired an off-duty Houston Police Department homicide detective to covertly watch the house and protect us if needed. My sisters made a slideshow with tons of pictures and music. The party was fabulous, but I worried the whole time.

The next day, Luke called wanting to meet me to discuss the binding arbitration that was set for that Wednesday in our divorce case. More than anything in the world, I wanted Luke to agree to terminate his rights to Gracie because then we could truly be free from him forever. So, I had to meet him and try to come to an agreement. I suggested we meet at Olive Garden, and I was already at a table when he arrived with Ryan. As soon as he sat down, Luke said, "You're going to give me $10,000, or I won't agree to terminate my rights to Gracie." I told him I did not have that amount of money, but he didn't believe me. I told him I would see what I could do and call him later.

In front of Ryan, he told me that I would *never* be safe from him. He further warned that even though he was forced to relinquish all his guns as part of the plea bargain, he could easily shoot me with a crossbow as I walked in the back dock of the courthouse. Sadly, I knew it was true. No one can truly protect me from him. That night, I had what would become a recurring nightmare of him killing me with a crossbow.

I called him later that day and told him I wasn't giving him 10,000 dollars. I told him that I had already done him a favor by keeping the years of abuse a secret. He replied, "I encourage you to take it public; this is the last time I'll talk to you, FUCKING WHORE."

That actually was the last time we ever spoke.

CHAPTER FOURTEEN

Fighting For Freedom

The next day, March 26, 2012, I was in a downtown Houston courtroom when I got a text message from Ryan that read, "Dad is talking about killing himself and taking me with him and I'm scared – Don't tell him I said this."

Despite the adoption, Luke viewed Ryan as only his son. I knew that if I did anything to take Ryan away from him, Luke would take things to another level. But, after this text, I had no choice; I had to do something. For Ryan to risk reaching out to me, clearly indicated things had escalated in his world. I knew that when I picked up Ryan from school, I could not bring him home with me. We would not be safe there.

I immediately left court and called Mom. I told her to start packing her car and explained we would load the rest in my car when I got home. My plan was to pick up Ryan and then go directly to a hotel so Luke couldn't find us. In the past, Luke had used Ryan's phone to text me. As I was driving, my mind was racing. I started thinking, "What if this is Luke's way of getting me to a specific location so he could shoot me with a crossbow?"

So, on the way to the school, I decided to stop by the police station. I told the officer what had happened and asked for a patrol car to be present in the parking lot when I went to the school. It turned into the biggest ordeal. I tried to explain the situation quickly, so I could pick up Ryan and get to the hotel. The officer I spoke with, took my urgency in a way that was unintended. Basically, he thought I was crazy. It was so frustrating to try to explain the gravity of the situation to someone who clearly thought I was a drama queen. I finally told him never mind and headed to the school.

When I got to Ryan's intermediate school, I was relieved to see multiple police cars and no Luke in the parking lot. I had already spoken with the school principal over the phone, who said he had Ryan in his office with the school counselor. When I went inside, the principal told me that Ryan had confided in him that he was afraid that Luke was going to kill him. As a precaution, school administrators put the school on "lockdown," which quickly made the news.

When Ryan and I got outside, the police officers separated us. One officer asked to see the text message on Ryan's phone, but of course, he deleted it after he sent it so Luke would not see it. Then there was this discussion (amongst the police officers) that maybe the text wasn't real, and Ryan never sent it!!! How could I get the text on my phone, if Ryan had never sent it? I was so mad and frustrated!

The officers wanted me to wait there in the school parking lot, while they went to Luke's house to talk to him. I told them I was going to a hotel, and I was not going to stand there in the parking lot like a sitting duck. Then they told me to go to the fire station around the block and wait there. Mom, Grace, Ryan and I waited for well over an hour only to find out that Luke told them that we just had lunch together the day before and that I was doing all of this to gain an advantage in the divorce. Shockingly, they believed it.

The officer told us we were "free to leave!" I was so angry and frustrated, but I didn't have time to entertain those emotions. We drove to a hotel sixty miles away in West Houston. My cousin was a hotel manager there and registered us under the fake name of Nancy Peacock. I felt safe that night for the first time in a very long time.

The next day, Jane Waters called and told me that Luke had been arrested for driving while intoxicated after hitting another car!! When the police arrived, Luke told them, "I'm an elected official and a police officer, and you should let me go." And they did! As he drove away, he immediately caused another accident because he had taken way too much Xanax. The officers then arrested him and took him to the hospital for a blood draw and then to the county jail, where Luke quickly bonded out.

Everyone knows the first rule of probation is don't get re-arrested. Because Luke had been arrested while he was on probation, Jane filed a motion to revoke his probation, causing a warrant for his arrest with a bond of $50,000. Luke had to post 10% to make the bond. For three very long days, Luke was AWOL - no one knew where he was. My mind was consumed with thoughts that Luke would finally go on the killing spree he had always talked about. And who would this killing spree include?

Although we continued to stay in hiding, I still had to go to court. If I didn't go to work, I didn't make money. But going to work meant he would know where to find me. So, I borrowed a car and entered the building through underground, secure locations Luke didn't have access to.

The Harris County Sheriff's Department, the agency he used to work for, issued a BOLO (be on the look-out) to all downtown police and deputies with Luke's booking photo and descriptors, explaining that he was currently wanted on a probation violation for a family violence case. The flyer further explained that he should be immediately detained, and under no circumstances, regardless of any credentials he may present, should he be allowed to bypass any screening station because he could attempt to gain entry to the building posing as law enforcement. There was great concern at the courthouse that if Luke were allowed in the building, without going through the metal detectors, he would enter with a gun, which left a host of scary options.

The next three days were long and took a toll on everyone, including my mother. We agreed that she would get up with Gracie in the middle of the night and give her a bottle, so I could get some rest. One night, I woke up to Gracie crying and my mom rocking her back and forth saying, "Fuck, fuck, fuck, fuck...." I took Gracie and asked her, "What in the hell is happening?" She started hysterically crying, "I HATE THAT MOTHERFUCKER! I'M GOING TO GO KILL HIM RIGHT NOW!"

She stormed out of the hotel room with her purse that had her gun in it! My mind was racing, and Grace was still screaming. I called her cell phone, and it rang on the coffee table. "Shit!" I thought, "Now my Mom is going to end up in jail!" Finally, about an hour later, she came back, explaining that she had been driving around. She was furious that we were the ones hiding and that she never saw any hint of abuse. It was at that moment when I realized all of this was happening to the people that loved me as much as it was happening to me, especially my mom.

Finally, Luke posted bond and a court date was set following week for the Judge to assess conditions of his release. At that court date, the Judge ordered that Luke wear a GPS device on his ankle, preventing him from coming near my house, Ryan's school, my office address or the courthouse, unless he had a scheduled court setting. The conditions also included that he have no contact with me whatsoever and no contact with Ryan, unless Ryan initiated the contact. Ryan sent him an email which read as follows:

Our Relationship   Inbox ×   🖶

                                                        ☆ ↩ ⋮

Our relationship has been strained for years, but the second you said you would kill me, our relationship was over. I guess what I am saying is that I don't want you to fight for custody over me. I don't want a relationship with you, you have done stuff to me in the past and I know your ways. You are a joke to me. If you take this [divorce] to trial, I will tear your you know what up. I have never truly loved you because of what you did to me. Our relationship is OVER. I am happier now than I have ever been. I have gained 13 pounds since last month because I have gotten the full meals you could not provide. You are not a proper dad and you never will be.

Prior to me taking Ryan, Luke had agreed to terminate his rights to Gracie, but the minute I left the school with Ryan, my divorce became extremely contested. My divorce attorney and friend, Stephanie Proffitt, received a call from Luke's divorce attorney who warned Stephanie that Luke was making threats against her and her staff. Luke's attorney felt Luke was an imminent danger, so he violated attorney-client privilege and warned Stephanie. She had also been told by one of her clients, who knew Luke's uncle, that Luke's family were all worried that he was going to kill me. I was pretty much frantic all the time, worrying about a Judge ordering me to share Gracie with him. Thank God Stephanie took my calls all hours of the night!

Because Luke was charged initially with only a misdemeanor, the maximum amount of time he could get on the probation revocation was up to one year in the county jail. At that time, the Sheriff gave misdemeanor inmates two days credit for every one day spent in jail due to overcrowding. The case had been reset a few times and by July, Luke was tired of paying for the GPS device and wanted to find out what was going to happen on the case. I knew Luke was in a dark place because he had recently resigned from his elected position, after public talk of legal proceedings to remove him from the position. Luke had no job, no source of income, and he was struggling to make the payments for his court-ordered GPS device.

This frustration came to a head on June 7, 2012, when Luke intentionally drove to my house, called me, and texted me to get a new warrant for his arrest. He knew once he was in jail, the case would be expedited. After an arrest warrant issued, Luke turned himself in to the jail. At the next court date, Luke asked that he be sentenced to time already served for the month he had spent in jail, waiting for the court date.

Jane objected and argued that one-month in jail was not sufficient for what he had done. Luke wanted out of jail, but he knew that if he didn't accept a deal from Jane, there would be a full-blown hearing and all of the documentation I collected would be heard in open court and admitted as evidence for the Judge to consider at sentencing. All the details of the years of his abuse would become public knowledge during a hearing. But still, Luke refused Jane's offer of 250 days and the case was set for a hearing.

On the day of the hearing, July 16, 2012, I was driving to court filled with anxiety. The fucked up hell that had become my life would now be talked about in open court in front of my colleagues and news media. I was almost to court when out of nowhere, a speeding SUV ran a red light and T-boned my car. The airbag punched me in the face so quickly that I didn't register what happened until after my car stopped spinning. The first thing I remember is another driver was yelling at the lady who ran the red light and hit me. Everyone was alright, but my car was not drivable. Jane sent an investigator to help me get to the courthouse. Initially, the investigator thought that Luke had caused the accident or tried to run me off the road, but it was just an accident. I grabbed Grace's car seat and we headed to court.

Because I didn't want to be in the same room as Luke, I waited in a witness room. Usually, I am privy to everything that happens in a courtroom, but not this time. My colleagues and friends kept me company while I waited outside. After what seemed like an eternity, Luke agreed to plead guilty to 250 days in jail, 100 less than the max! At 2 for 1 credit, he would only serve 95 more days. His release date was scheduled for early October.

I felt like a could breathe again and take my constant hyper-vigilant state down a few notches. In the next few months, I felt so safe. I just had to get through the divorce, and then this would all be over. I assumed Luke would use this time in jail to calm down and reflect.

CHAPTER FIFTEEN

Like a Knife Through Butter

O ver the summer, I started talking to my old friend, Todd Trlicek more frequently. I needed a metal gazebo I ordered online assembled, so I told him if he helped me put it together, my mom would cook dinner for all three of us. We had a good time and got the gazebo put together. I learned later Todd hates salmon, but he ate every bite. This was the first time I had seen him in years, and it felt nice to reconnect. He came over for dinner with us another time, and we texted frequently.

And then finally, we went out on a date. Todd got us tickets for a concert at a country bar to hear John Conlee perform. We had a great time. I had not been country dancing since before I met Luke. It was so much fun. At the end of the night we kissed, and I felt like a teenager again. I wanted to feel that way every day!

We continued to see each other often. Mom and I got into a huge fight because she said it was too soon and that I needed to "find myself" again before I dated anyone. I had moved back into the marital home, where I was living the night of the Christmas party incident. Mom moved in with me to help with Gracie. I wanted to see Todd, but I didn't want any conflict with anyone, let alone my mom. So, after she went to bed, I would literally sneak Todd in my bathroom window. I was 40 years old, living in my own house, and sneaking a boy into my room. We laugh about it now.

At one point, I remember telling Todd not to fall in love with me because I was just using him for sex. He laughed and kept being wonderful. Mom ended up moving back to her house, and Todd moved in with me. We loved being together, and it was my house. So, I decided that if I changed my mind, I could just tell him to leave whenever I wanted. But I was having fun and I really needed to feel the way he made me feel.

The divorce proceedings continued, and Ryan mailed a letter to Luke in jail, which read:

> Dad, I love you, but I don't want to see you. You have said threats in the past and I don't want to take the chance of them being more than threats. I don't want to see you. If that changes, I will let you know. If you truly love me, then you will respect what I want and terminate your rights.

Luke wrote me two letters from jail. He claimed, "Jail has given me time to reflect on the things I have done and pain I have caused, and I am truly sorry. I am glad I was able to plead and keep you from having to relive any painful event." He admitted, "I don't know what I said to Ryan while I freaked out on Xanax." He warned, "If we can't agree on the divorce, we will go to trial and I'll end up paying 25% in child support, but I WILL get visitation to Gracie." Then he boasted that the County Judge "came to see me, as he does every two weeks, and he told me that you wrecked your car." In saying this, Luke was making sure I understood that he had the support of elected officials and that he still knew what was happening in my life. I did not respond to his letters.

The summer flew by. In late September, days before Luke was scheduled to be released from the county jail, I was at a hearing to obtain a two-year protective order against Luke. Judy, Luke's first wife, agreed to explain to the Judge the abuse she had endured from Luke during their marriage. I was so thankful to her. Her testimony allowed the Judge to come to a decision without requiring Ryan's testimony. Ryan was upset because he wanted to testify, but I was relieved.

While there at the courthouse, Luke's cousin, Russell, called me and told me not to go forward with the protective order. Luke told Russell he was going to kill me if I got the protective order. Because Luke was in jail, I knew anything he said was recorded. So, I called Jane and she pulled the audio of the jail calls. Stephanie also subpoenaed the calls to use in the divorce case.

When I listened to the recorded phone calls, I expected to hear him saying that I'm a "bitch" or that he wished I was dead. But instead, I heard the calm and calculating tone of his voice detail his specific thoughts on how he planned to kill me. In a conversation with his half-brother (one of the twins), he acknowledged, "Well if I kill her, I'll get the death penalty."

In another conversation with his cousin Russell, he was initially hesitant to verbalize how he wanted to kill me but eventually opened up. When Luke found out that Ryan was talking to investigators and prosecutors about him, he responded, "I can't believe Ryan, that lying MOTHER FUCKER." He then directed his anger at me asking, "What can I do to that bitch? I think I should kill her. I can sit on the feeder road and light her car up with an AR15. Bullets like a knife through butter! I wish that fucking cunt was reasonable. How much do you let someone push you? She has pushed me and given me no choice. I'm gonna have to finish it."

There was another conversation with James, who at the time was an active duty police officer, where Luke admitted, "I've talked to Russell and the issue is, do I kill her or not? I had such high expectations and you do this; it makes me dangerous. She knows what she is doing would make a reasonable person angry (referring to my getting the protective order). I'll be out in a week." Although Russell had a strong moral compass and contacted me with concern, James never told anyone about the threats Luke made on my life.

Over the next several days, I frantically tried to prepare for Luke's release. My bedroom window faced the front of the house, and the street came to a dead end into our driveway at the center of the cul-de-sac. I was scared that Luke would drive his car through the house and into my bed, so I bought a huge boulder and had it positioned in front of my bedroom window. I also moved the head of the bed to a different wall and had three thick sheets of plywood, thick enough to stop bullets, drilled over my bedroom window. I had a high-tech, eight-camera security system installed around the house.

I borrowed military combat grade bullet-proof vests (and helmets) from numerous friends for myself and family members. I felt safer wearing the vest and helmet when I drove. I always kept one draped over Gracie's car seat. I realize this sounds extreme, but I was convinced Luke was going to shoot up my car as he had threatened. I was pissed at myself for having fun all summer when I should have been preparing for Luke's release. I should have known the calmness of the summer was too good to be true.

Luke had been sitting in jail for months on the probation violation from the assault case and then days before his release, he was describing in detail how he was going to kill me. But there was nothing Luke could be charged with because he didn't communicate an immediate threat directly to me. Jane and Bill Exley (my dear friend and also a prosecutor), were convinced that Luke's threats were imminent and that despite the passage of months, he was going to hurt me when he got out of jail.

Bill and Jane believed numerous more serious crimes had occurred, but these crimes happened out of their jurisdiction. So, they decided to go visit officials in the county where we lived when Luke assaulted me during my pregnancy. This meant a different prosecutor would have to decide if Luke had committed any state crime. Bill and Jane took all the documentation that I saved to the District Attorney in that county. The DA took all of my documentation to a grand jury, allowing the grand jury to determine whether there was sufficient evidence to file any charge against Luke.

On October 10, 2012, the grand jury indicted Luke with aggravated assault with a deadly weapon, for the April 9, 2011 incident which occurred when I was seven months pregnant. Instead of Luke being released from Harris County jail as scheduled, he was transferred by bus to the other county. His bond was set at $200,000 on the new aggravated assault case. Somehow, he got a bonding company to take less than the standard ten percent and accept only $5,000 on the $200,000 bond. He made bond quickly.

Russell, Luke's cousin, borrowed the money to bond Luke out of jail. Luke moved in with Russell, which gave Russell an opportunity to observe Luke's state of mind. It didn't take long for Russell to realize he made a mistake by posting Luke's bond.

One day, Russell asked me to meet him in a parking lot because he didn't want to talk over the phone. Russell confided in me that Luke was talking freely with him about killing me, but that he was more focused on killing Layla, my sister. Luke told Russell that he wanted me to suffer and that killing my sister, a mother of six kids, would definitely achieve that goal. I called the prosecutor and told him that Luke was becoming more unstable, and Russell was willing to give a recorded statement about the threats Luke had been making. Everyone was in high alert mode.

Todd is a Marine Corps veteran and former police officer, so being close to him made me feel a little safer, but I was still a hot mess. I slept with a gun under my pillow. Todd was also there with his gun ready, but having my own gun provided me some comfort. I went to court in the mornings and came straight home. Gracie stayed at home with Mom because I didn't want her leaving the house. I told Mom she always had to have her gun ready. She did.

There were numerous alerts triggered due to Luke coming within a restricted area or not charging the GPS unit. These alerts sent everyone into frantic mode because he was either "off the grid" again or going near a protected address. One of these occasions, I received an alert Luke was near my house. I called 9-1-1 and hid in my closet with my gun and Gracie. Not long after that incident, the police department sent out SWAT officers to draw a diagram of the house to use in the event of a hostage situation. I gave the police department unrestricted remote access to my eight-camera security system.

The day after Christmas, SWAT was beating on my door at 6:00 AM. After looking through the peep-hole, Todd opened the door in his underwear. There were cops everywhere holding AR-style weapons. Luke's GPS was not pinging, and they were concerned he was coming over to my house. Many other times his GPS would ping in the exclusion zone around

Layla's or my Dad's house. One time, Gracie was at Layla's when I was notified of a ping very near her house. I frantically called Layla and told her to get ready. There was no reason for him to be anywhere near there.

He would always claim these violations were accidental. Finally, the Judge admonished him that if there were any more violations, he would send Luke back to jail. Things were quiet after that.

The divorce proceedings dragged on for what seemed like an eternity. A Judge from a different county was specially assigned to preside over the divorce proceedings. I was not willing to settle for anything less than no contact with him for the rest of my life, which meant there could be no joint custody agreement.

Child Protective Services conducted an investigation finding there was physical abuse to Ryan. Ryan's therapist wrote a letter to the court explaining Ryan's request for Luke's rights to be terminated. The custody case was set for trial, but Luke ultimately agreed to terminate his parental rights to *both* Ryan and Gracie. I was overjoyed but knew the Judge still had to agree that the terminations were in the best interest of the children. In Texas, termination is extremely rare, unless there is a simultaneous adoption. The theory being courts don't want to bastardize children. (*Oh, the irony...*) Thankfully the Judge agreed that terminating Luke's parental rights was in the best interest of both children.

The divorce was final. The entire family celebrated! I was ecstatic that Luke would never be able to hurt any of us again. I knew termination was the best way to keep the kids safe, but I dreaded the day I had to explain to Gracie all that happened.

The criminal case ended up in a court where the Judge knew Luke, so he recused himself. Again, a special judge from another county was assigned to preside over the criminal matter. I told the prosecutor I did not want to go to trial. Now that Luke's rights were terminated, I didn't care what happened to the criminal case. This made everyone in my family angry because they all thought he should be in prison at least, preferably dead. But I was still afraid of Luke completely snapping.

Luke had been an elected official with a law degree and was now working at a chemical plant. A job he could not keep if he was convicted of a felony. He had already lost so much, all of which he already blamed me for. If he lost what little he had left, he would have nothing left to live for and I would be dead for sure. I pleaded with the prosecutor to offer deferred probation. My thinking was that Luke could move on more easily without a felony conviction.

Initially, the prosecutor only offered prison time, but finally agreed to offer 8-year deferred adjudication probation. Luke refused the offer, and everyone was preparing for trial. In the final hour, he changed his mind and accepted the deferred probation. As a condition, he was required to wear an ankle monitor for the first 2½ years of the probation.

Luke had a new girlfriend, and Russell would keep me up-to-date with their relationship status because every time she broke up with him, Luke became very unstable. Russell wanted me to keep my guard up during these times. The last time they broke up, Russell and I were convinced that the relationship was over for good. But they ended up getting back together after she found out she was pregnant.

They moved in together and their twin girls were born soon after. I wondered if she was going through the same things I had. I also thought about the new babies and worried about their future. But most of all, I felt relief that he had moved on.

I was able to find comfort in that he had a new family to focus on and would hopefully forget about me and everything that happened between us. I still didn't like to go out to eat for fear I would see him. We lived near each other, and I hated that because I was constantly looking over my shoulder. This anxiety lingered over me because I was still afraid of Luke and his instability.

During the probation, everything was quiet until the prosecutor told me he was trying to get off probation early so he could move to another state. I told the prosecutor that I would agree to the early termination if Luke agreed to a lifetime protective order for Grace and me. Luke agreed, signed the life-time protective order and his probation was early terminated after about five years.

Luke moved away from Texas and the state he chose for his new home was, I'm sure, a product of research on which state would still give him a law license after his three arrests and three plea bargains. When he had studied for the bar the first time, he begged me to take the prep course with him and help him study. This was impossible because the prep course lasted most of the day and I had to work. So, when I found out that his new wife was in law school, this made perfect sense. By the time she finished law school, he would be off probation and he could potentially sit for the bar exam in that state. And he would not have to study by himself.

I don't know his new wife, so I don't know if she ever had any intention of going to law school before she met him. I doubt that moving cross country, leaving her family here and starting law school was something she had envisioned prior to meeting Luke. It's almost like Luke was trying to recreate his life and pick up where things started going badly for him legally. I even heard rumors of him wanting to run for office in his new hometown.

You may think it strange but today, I can honestly say I harbor no ill will towards Luke. It took me years to mentally get to a point where I literally do not care what happens to him. I don't care whether he is successful or whether he has an amazing career, as long as I never have to see him again.

CHAPTER SIXTEEN

The Calm After the Storm

My life now is so amazing that sometimes I think I'm dreaming. Todd and I married in a beautiful ceremony in October of 2014. He adopted Grace when she was three, and she loves him so much. I literally could not ask for a better father or husband. As it turns out, Todd was adopted by his father also, making the bond between the two, extra special. Todd is such a good human and father that sometimes I think I don't deserve him or the wonderful way he treats me. But then I remind myself that the way he makes me feel is the way all relationships should be, functional and loving.

Grace is eight now, going on twenty-five. She won't tolerate being called Gracie anymore because it sounds like a baby's name. She is beautiful, freaky smart, and makes me laugh constantly. Many might focus on the trauma and tragedy I experienced, but I love my life, and I would go through everything with Luke a hundred more times to be where I am today.

The one thing I still struggle with is the lapse in my judge of character. I have always prided myself on my ability to read people and rely on my gut instincts. Luke was able to get past me. In addition to many suspected undiagnosed mental disorders, Luke was a textbook narcissist and master manipulator. He was not a good person, but I didn't see that. Abusers can be very charismatic and charming in the beginning, until you fall in love, which makes leaving a more difficult decision.

Now that I have fully revealed the entire truth, I know exactly how blessed I truly am. But inevitably, I get the dreaded question, "But, why did you stay?" For years I had an extremely hard time answering the question. A friend from high school asked me, "Why didn't you just leave?" I became so filled with rage that I almost screamed at her. She loves me and didn't mean to pass judgment, but her inability to understand why leaving was not that simple made me angry. A question like this makes a victim feel judged.

Hopefully, by now, you understand leaving is not simple, for any woman. Every woman's situation is different. Some don't have the financial resources to leave, while others are too scared to leave. Domestic violence happens across all socioeconomic levels of society. It's everywhere. Don't assume that because someone is emotionally strong, that abuse couldn't be happening to them. The truth is, you never know what's going on behind closed doors. To get a loved one out of an abusive relationship, be prepared to support and accept them in ways that you may not be comfortable with.

There is one commonality for all abused women, it's shame and fear of judgment that comes with being labeled a victim. There is shame in "allowing" yourself to be abused. The fear of judgment is most often too heavy to bear, so the secret stays a secret. The judgment makes women feel like something is wrong with them because a "normal person" wouldn't allow themselves to be beaten. For me, one of the main reasons I never told anyone anything bad about Luke is because I knew my family and friends would tell me to get out of the relationship, and I wasn't emotionally ready to give up on my marriage. I knew they would judge him, which would make our family dynamics more difficult, so I kept *everything* a secret.

How can you support an abused woman? Be the opposite of their abuser. Don't add more pressure to her life by trying to force her to leave the relationship. She's already under intense pressure and wants to believe that things will get better. Don't try to make her follow your timetable because standing up to an abuser is terrifying. Instead, discuss options with her, and let her know you are always available. If she is not ready to leave and you pass judgment on her decision, she will no longer confide in you, and possibly, shut you out completely.

Also, avoid comments that sound condescending, like "You are too smart to allow this to happen," or "I would get out if this was happening to me." Don't act like you know everything about her life, because you don't! And no matter how hard you try, remember, you don't know what she is feeling. You can empathize, but you have no idea. Listen more and talk less. Respect her decisions, even if you don't agree with them. Think "with her" not "for her." This may create frustration for you. Constantly remind yourself that it's about *her*, not you.

I truly hope my experience creates awareness not just about domestic violence, but also awareness about how extremely difficult it is to leave an abuser. I hope my account will inspire mothers to talk to their daughters, not just warn them to leave when there is violence but to also make sure they understand the red flags and promise to confide in someone when red flags appear. Recognizing red flags, and not dismissing them, is the most important factor in domestic violence intervention.

I hope my experience allows women to be better moms, sisters, and friends and to notice and ask questions when they observe isolation or inexplicable changes in behavior or mood. I also hope that men read this book and strive to be better partners and to raise better men. Remember that an abused woman probably already feels shame, fear, and confusion and she will likely need someone to counteract those negative feelings and thoughts. You can help her best by being that person.

FROM THE FAMILY

As close as we are, I kept these dark secrets from my sisters and my parents for more than six years. We held family dinners and parties, celebrated Christmas and Thanksgiving each year, and even vacationed together. Through all of that, you would think they would have either noticed the signs or would have been suspicious of possible trouble in my home.

When speaking with others about the experience I went through, my sister, Katie, shares how things looked from her perspective; and how my family never knew, or even suspected the personal terror that I suffered during the marriage.

Katie shares:

How did I respond to the news? Complete disbelief. I was pulling into the parking garage at work when my mom called me early that morning. I was in complete and total disbelief as she told me all that transpired with my sister the night before. As I looked at the picture of her battered and broken face in the text message, I just couldn't make sense of it. That image and the events my mom described simply did not add up with the person I knew as my big sister, Mekisha. Honestly, if asked to name the strongest women I knew, Mekisha would have undoubtedly topped my list. All her life, Mekisha had never let people walk on her or push her around. She was her own person and didn't take crap from anyone. Of all people, how could SHE be a victim of domestic violence? And not just one incident, but violence and terror spanning YEARS?

As I reflect on this question almost eight years later, I am still deeply disappointed and regretful that I never put the pieces together. We are a very close family and spend time together often. My two sisters, my parents, and I all live within 15 miles of one another - we aren't the kind of family who gets together only once or twice a year. We are frequently in touch with each other by phone, text, and email, and we keep up with what's going on in each other's lives. We help each other. We share genuine laughter and love. So how in the world could we not see what Luke had done to Mekisha for years, right underneath our noses?

The bottom line is - Mekisha didn't want us to know. She feared for her safety (and ours), and she did all that she could to keep the secret. Mekisha's strength made her an extraordinary actress. She is highly intelligent and strategic, thinking ahead and anticipating how to explain away any oddity that may be questioned.

Did we think Luke was a good husband? No, we did not. Even without knowledge of the abuse, we knew that Luke was a terrible husband. We knew the cruel names he called her, his refusal to stay anywhere but a lavish hotel room, and how selfish he was, like spending money on a Corvette when they could not afford it. We knew Mekisha deserved better, we all agreed that if she was happy with him, then we should be happy for her. After all, the family wasn't married to him - SHE was. And if being his wife made her happy, then why should we take that from her? Did we tell her that? Absolutely not. Collectively, we agreed to support her by putting our personal feelings of him aside and focusing on - what we thought was - her happiness.

I remember several of the incidents that seemed insignificant at the time, but now, knowing the context of the big picture, were immensely critical signs of something terrible happening in my sister's life. For example, Mekisha told us she kept a personal journal in her office Downtown. She said that if anything should happen to her, we needed to get her journal. At the time, this sounded weird. BUT, Mekisha is like a family historian - documenting the events and cataloging the keepsakes. She's been this way all our lives. So, for her to say she had a journal in her office for us to retrieve if she died, it just seemed like "over the top" Mekisha making sure we would keep her memories and reflections as part of the historical family records. Given this, and the nonchalant way she mentioned it, it just didn't seem strange. Of course, now, I see it was like a cannon in the night that should have signaled great trouble.

In another situation, Mekisha was in a car accident while she was pregnant with Grace. She called me right after the accident, upset and worrying about the baby's well-being. I suggested that she go to the doctor's office just to get checked out and be on the safe side. We stayed on the phone, and as we talked more, she explained that when she told Luke about the accident, he was angry with her. He wasn't worried about his wife or the baby's health; he was worried about the car and the insurance rates. I was also pregnant, and I couldn't fathom a husband responding that way. But, instead of focusing on that, I focused on how I could support my sister at that moment. I drove to her doctor's office and was in the room with her while they checked on the baby. During the exam, Luke wordlessly entered the room. He didn't comfort Mekisha or apologize for his reaction. He just stood there awkwardly. I felt they deserved privacy, so I left the office, knowing that Mekisha and the baby were healthy, and her husband was here for her now. Of course, now I regret those choices. Why didn't I ask her if their marriage was okay? Why didn't I ask her if she felt safe at home? Why did I just let him off the hook and leave it just between them? That was not normal! I knew he was cruel and insensitive, but I never thought Mekisha would be trapped in such violence. Not her!

I want to share my perspective with those who read this book because no one should ever assume that this couldn't happen to them or someone they love. <u>It is not a matter of strength.</u> Women who are abused are not weak. While I never thought that consciously, I clearly had an unconscious belief that some women were "too strong" to let any man abuse them (like Mekisha). I could not have been more wrong. And if I hadn't held that unconscious belief, could she have gotten out sooner and suffered less? Maybe. Maybe not.

I wish she hadn't felt so isolated and alone. If I could have at least been a confidant and a comfort to her, perhaps that would have eased her suffering a small amount. I know you can't look back, and you can't change the past, but today I'm only grateful she and Grace made it out of that situation alive. It's terrifying how many people don't, and I'm proud of my sister for what she accomplished.

Looking back, I feel foolish for thinking I was alone because I was not. Despite his forgiveness, I continue to feel an extreme amount of guilt for failing Ryan in so many ways. But the years of emotional abuse left me "mind-fucked" where I believed all of Luke's threats. I felt trapped when I wasn't. I had income, family, friends and endless resources at my fingertips. I was educated, financially stable, but still could not break free. It's like I was in a flat spin and couldn't see which way was up.

Today, I have completely healed emotionally. And I owe this to my husband, my family, and friends who supported me nonstop. For years, I blamed myself for not leaving sooner. When I finally accepted what happened as the past, I was able to move forward and heal emotionally. If you've read this and question if you'll be able to heal and move on, trust me you will!

But, Why Did You Stay?

AUTHOR BIO

Mekisha Jane Walker

Mekisha was raised in Houston, Texas, by her parents with her two sisters, in a normal middle class childhood. After she graduated from college, she continued to law school. Upon graduation from law school, she was offered a position as a prosecutor at the Harris County District Attorney's office, fulfilling a childhood dream to become prosecutor. Mekisha was successful in her career and became a successful criminal trial attorney. But she had a secret, a secret she never confided in anyone. Her husband verbally and physically abused her, and she concealed it from everyone in her life. As a former prosecutor, she had extensive resources available, but she was still unable to break free. It was not until the abuse publicly escalated that her secret was finally revealed. She remained unbroken and finally summoned the strength to escape the cruel and violent relationship that had become her daily reality. Mekisha created a new life, one free from abuse, and now shares her experiences to create awareness and inspire hope for people currently trapped in a violent relationship.

Author Contact Information

Email: mjw@butwhydidyoustay.com

Website: www.butwhydidyoustay.com

Facebook: @butwhydidyoustay

Instagram: @butwhydidyoustay

If you haven't taken advantage of my interactive website www.butwhydidyoustay.com, that chronicles the indepthness of each individual chapter with photos, videos, transcripts, news articles, and live voice recordings, please log on and subscribe today.